Create
Impressive
Documents

Steve Hards

≋ *briarwood 1000* ≋

Text and diagrams © 1996 by
Steve Hards

For stylistic reasons, this
edition is not for sale outside
the United Kingdom.

First published in 1996 by
Briarwood 1000.

ISBN 0 9528776 0 0

Catalogue category: Word
Processing. Key words:
typography; graphic design;
desktop publishing.

Printed in Bury St Edmunds,
Suffolk, by Miro Press.

The examples on pages 145 – 149
are reproduced with permission of
Bexley and Greenwich Health.

Windows is a trademark of
Microsoft Corporation. All other
trademarks acknowledged.

Create Impressive Documents

Contents

Dedication and Acknowledgements

This book is dedicated to all the secretaries alongside whom I have worked in the course of my management consultancy in recent years. They are too numerous to name, but without exception they won my admiration for their struggles to get to grips with the intricacies of word processing, the quirks of software and tiresome computer manuals. To them I would like to say: *Thank you for your patience with my interruptions and requests and, by the way, this book sets down all the things I tried to explain from time to time!*

The book is also dedicated to Grace George, the art teacher who taught me that understanding what you are looking at is an important part of its enjoyment.

I acknowledge a debt of thanks to colleagues who, over the years, have nudged me into improving my skills on document presentation. They often contributed directly to my learning and in particular, I would like to thank:
Bernard Payne, Caroline Lovejoy, Debbie Phillipson and Debby Baker.

I also thank Tim Hards for his relentless eagle-eyed proof-reading and Debbie Phillipson for her invaluable editorial advice. Any faults that finally slipped through are mine!

SH

The Start of a Journey

Have you watched someone preparing a car for sale? The car gets the best clean inside that it has ever had: every cranny is vacuumed and every mark wiped off. Why?

A Chinese proverb says 'If you haven't got a smile, don't be a shopkeeper'.

In the case of the car a good impression adds value in the eyes of potential buyers and boosts the confidence of the seller. The shopkeeper's smile costs nothing, but the impression it makes can be the difference between failure and success.

Think how much effort is put into producing reports, letters, leaflets, brochures and other documents where you work. They are probably drafted, redrafted, consulted upon and revised to get the content, the words and the phrases right. Yet all that effort is undermined if the documents that arrive in the readers' hands look poor. By contrast, good-looking reports that are weak in content can make a greater impact than they deserve. Imagine, therefore, the power of a report that is strong on content *and* presentation. Making a good impression with your documents is not difficult: you just need to know how.

This book will teach you. It does not matter which word processing or desktop publishing software you use, the principles are the same and the things you will learn by working through this book will outlast many changes in software design.

I have divided the book into six sections. To get you started I have put all the things that can be done quickly into the first part, *Quick Bits*. The things you will want to master when your appetite for improving your documents has grown are carefully sequenced in the following sections — you will therefore get maximum benefit by working through each section in turn.

This book assumes that you know how to do the basics with your word processor, so the emphasis is always on *why* to do things rather than *how* to do them. It is a guide book to the interesting places on your route to the creation of impressive documents. Have a good journey!

Steve Hards

Word processor warning!

Not all word processors, particularly old and non-Windows software, will do all of the things featured in this book. However, applying the principles as far as you can will still improve the look of your documents. Sometimes, when you know what you want to do, you can work out other methods of achieving the effects.

You can be assured that I practice what I preach. Everything you see in this book went straight to the printers from my office laser printer via my personal computer using *Microsoft Word (Version 6)* word processing software.

Examination warning!

I was prompted to write this book because in the course of my work as a management consultant I come across so many poorly presented reports. I am not a typing teacher. If you are taking an exam in typing or word processing *please* produce things in the way you are being taught, otherwise you may not pass! I have studied publications relating to these exams and they seem to be intent on perpetuating the idea that word processors are only sophisticated typewriters. They are not. As this book will radically change the way that you treat your word processed documents, may I reluctantly suggest that you put it away until you pass your exams. It will not be too late then to become someone who enjoys improving his or her documents by the intelligent application of typographic and design principles.

Part 1. Quick Bits

In this section you will learn many ways to make the next document you work on look more impressive. The changes themselves are quick and easy to make but, just because they look small and can be done quickly, never underestimate their importance. When they are all put together they make quite a difference. In the later sections of the book you will learn about the more dramatic changes you can make.

Most people assume that the way to make documents visually impressive is to use layouts with fancy margins, interesting fonts and graphics. The big secret is, in fact, to pay close attention to the detail and to be consistent throughout the document. This section explains the detail to look out for.

It may take two or three hours to work through *Quick Bits* because sometimes it takes a while to explain why certain changes have the effect they do.

1.1 Making a start

Work through the book in chunks at your own pace with an already-typed document in front of you on the screen:

- Find a document about eight pages long. Ideally, it should already be divided into parts by headings and contain a few, but only a few, tables.
- Save the file under another name. This is the one we will use from now on, to experiment with.
- If the document is longer than ten pages, or if it only has tables after that point, copy one or two tables, bring them forward to earlier pages (your experimental document does not have to make sense!) and delete page nine onwards.
- Print out a copy before you change it, for future reference.
- If your word processor cannot show on the screen some of the characters we will be using you may want to print a page from time to time to check that what you are doing comes out correctly, but please resist printing the *whole* document until I let you know.
- Save your new document as you go along, so that you can come back to it if you have a break.

You may want to read ahead before you start but you will understand the principles more quickly and remember the points more easily by reading and making changes to your document at the same time. If you *do* read ahead, please go back and make the changes later.

This book is not written for a specific word processor. If you keep your software manual handy it will tell you whether and how your word processor does the things suggested.

You may want to read ahead before you start but you will understand the principles more quickly and remember the points more easily by reading and making changes to your document at the same time. If you *do* read ahead, please go back and make the changes later.

1.2. Showing emphasis

When we write things by hand we emphasise points by underlining. When typewriters were invented the practice of underlining was copied. Apart from using capital letters, this was all that most typewriters could do. When typewriter technology eventually enabled such things as bold effects and changeable typefaces, we were already moving into the word processor era.

Professional printers use italic or bold text for emphasis. It makes the point, but distracts the eye less. So now, when you next type up a hand-written text and see something underlined, be like someone who sets type: use italics. (Do not do anything to your document yet.) If something is strongly emphasised, use bold.

Italic emphasis is *normal.*
Bold is the equivalent of shouting.
Bold italics are *over the top!*

Some people use capital letters (also called 'upper case letters' from the time when printers kept metal type in wooden cases) for emphasis. But the proper use of capitals is a whole subject in itself, so it has its own section. Just promise yourself that from now on, you will never use capitals or underlining to emphasise text.

When using italic or bold text it is good practice to use an italic or bold space in front of the first word that is changed, otherwise the printed space may appear either too small or too big depending on your software, the font you are using and the particular combination of letters involved. Use a non-italic or non-bold space where the changes end. How do you get an italic or bold space? The same way as you do with text: select it and mark it as italic or bold.

What to do now

Search* your document for words and phrases that are emphasised by using underlining or capitals. Change them to non-capital (lower case) italic or bold type as you think appropriate.

If you do not find anything to change, identify a few phrases that you can emphasise for practice.

---

* In the rest of the book, when it says search or find use your word processor's 'Find', 'Replace' or 'Search and Replace' facility. Otherwise, use your eyes.

When it comes to making a good impression, getting the detail right is more important than the overall layout!

1.3. Managing quotations

Italic text

As well as for emphasis, italic text is the preferred way to set out short quotations. See the two examples at the top of the opposite page.

Did you notice that when italics are used for quotations, quotation marks (also known as inverted commas) are not needed around the text?

Long quotations need different handling because large blocks of italic text are difficult to read. As a rule of thumb, 'large' is text that runs over three lines or more. Here, quotation marks are preferred. Compare the third and fourth examples opposite.

If the quotation runs to more than one paragraph, the convention is to give each paragraph a quotation mark *only* at its beginning, so that the reader knows that the quotation is continuing, and to reserve the closing quotation mark for the end of the last paragraph.

In typography (the art of setting type), unfamiliar foreign words, the titles of books, magazines, poems, songs, etc. are treated as if they were short quotations, so use italics in preference to quotation marks.

She stopped eating the *paratha.*
After watching *Pride and Prejudice* many viewers bought the book.
The song *The Sloop John B.* was popular in the Bahamas by the 1920s.

Passing references to inanimate objects that are given names, such as trains, aeroplanes and ships are treated in the same way. However, if you were writing an article about such an object that referred to it frequently by name, readers would become irritated if it were constantly italicised. In that case it would be better treated as normal text.

Whether there was actually a sloop called *John B.* is open to question.
The space probe *Galileo* is sending back amazing pictures.

Short quotations

I recall Harold Wilson saying on television, *It does not mean, of course, that the pound here in Britain, in your pocket or purse or in your bank has been devalued.*

In his book about Spain, first published in ~~published in~~ 1906, Edward Hutton says of Fuenterrabia: *Figure to yourself a little city set on a hill, above a river with a name so beautiful as the Bidasoa.* We might now call it a small town, but its charm is undiminished.

Long quotations

Edward Hutton said of Fuenterrabia: *Figure to yourself a little city set on a hill, above a river with a name so beautiful as the Bidasoa. The streets are too steep and too stony for any wheeled traffic, and the sun is almost excluded by the roofs and balconies of the houses...on that Sunday afternoon those shadowy streets were full of women and children passing from church to church; the women wearing the black mantilla, which is so much more charming than any hat can ever be.*

Edward Hutton said of Fuenterrabia: 'Figure to yourself a little city set on a hill, above a river with a name so beautiful as the Bidasoa. The streets are too steep and too stony for any wheeled traffic, and the sun is almost excluded by the roofs and balconies of the houses...on that Sunday afternoon those shadowy streets were full of women and children passing from church to church; the women wearing the black mantilla, which is so much more charming than any hat can ever be.'

Quotation marks

Quotation marks are used to enclose direct quotations or speech when, for some reason, italics are not appropriate. They are not used when the quotation or speech is just reported, as in the second of each of the first two examples opposite.

Modern preference is to use single ('...') rather than double ("...") quotation marks whenever possible. The most important thing, whether using italics or quotation marks, is to be consistent throughout the document.

Quotation marks have other uses, relating to an author's need to single out words without emphasising them. To indicate, for example, that he or she considers that:

- A word is unacceptable in some way — slang, or not as formal as the rest of the writing.
- Its use or meaning is not fully established.
- The writer disagrees with someone else's use of the word.
- The words need to be separated out because they are being explained.

Quotations within quotations

Some quotations enclose others. If italics are used for the main quotation, the embedded one is enclosed with single quotation marks. If single marks are in use, then double ones are used, and vice versa, as shown in these examples.

Punctuation before quotations

Most people are taught to put a comma before direct speech but you can use a range of marks depending on the urgency of what is being conveyed. Readers mentally pause for increasing lengths of time in the following sequence: no mark, comma, semicolon, colon, full stop.

Direct speech and quotations

Michelle asked Paul, 'What are you doing in my room?'

Michelle asked Paul what he was doing in her room.

Jackson wrote '...it is *outrageous* that dancing should be allowed.'

Jackson wrote that it was *outrageous* (his emphasis) that dancing should be allowed.

Singling out words

She was the 'sexiest' woman he had ever met.

Why on earth do some people think shopping is a 'sexy' activity?

He said that 'crisis situations' were caused by failures of management.

What Americans call 'potato chips', the English call 'crisps'.

Quotations within quotations

Jackson wrote: *According to Hayes, '...it is outrageous that dancing should be allowed' but I do not agree.* We concur.

Jackson wrote: 'According to Hayes, "...it is outrageous that dancing should be allowed" but I do not agree.' We concur.

Jackson wrote: "According to Hayes, '...it is outrageous that dancing should be allowed' but I do not agree." We concur.

Curved quotation marks

When you need to use quotation marks, how do you get proper curved ones and not the little straight marks ('...') that computer keyboards have kept from typewriter days? Increasingly, modern software can automatically replace straight ones with the appropriate curved ones, depending on whether they are at the beginning or end of the word. If your software does not have that facility, you can still print curved ones. It is just a little more fiddly, but worth it to make a good impression. The text opposite explains how.

What to do now

Back to your document that has been waiting for its next 'treatment'!

Search for text in quotation marks. If you use a 'find' facility, search for the straight double quotation mark first (") and the single straight quotation mark (') next. For now, ignore the apostrophes that this will pick up. Change any straight quotation marks to curved ones.

Next, review the text changing it into italics where appropriate, or sorting out the quotation marks according to the above principles.

No quotations in the text of your document? Make some up!

Accessing non-keyboard characters

Word processors can produce many more characters than there are keys on the keyboard. Examples are:

‡ ‰ Œ § ½ ¿ Ñ Ø ç þ é ü ß

Your word processor may allow you to access 'non-keyboard' characters in several ways:

- In most Windows software, a single curved quotation mark for the beginning, with its tail up (') is accessed by the keystrokes Alt+0145 and the quotation mark at the end, with its tail down (') by Alt+0146. That is, you hold down the Alt key and type in 0145 or 0146 on the number pad: it does not work with the numbers at the top of the keyboard.

- If you do not get the right (or any) character, you will need to refer to your manual or on-screen help to sort out which keystrokes you need, but the principle will be the same. In the DOS version of WordPerfect, for example, the codes that correspond to the above are: Ctrl v 0,96 for (') and Ctrl v 0,39 for (').

- You may be able to set up your keyboard to produce the required characters quickly when you need them. Your software manual will tell you how.

- With a Windows-based program you may be able to identify the character from a menu that inserts things into the text. In Word, for example, you access 'Insert' and 'Symbol'. Alternatively, you can fetch it from the program called Character Map.

- In non-Windows programs look in your manual for 'characters', 'symbols' or 'international characters' and how to insert them.

Learning keystrokes to insert common non-keyboard characters is worth doing as it is quicker than getting them from pull-down menus. I have spent some time explaining this process because we will soon use this facility again for other characters.

If you can only use curved quotation marks by accessing the character set through a menu and you have lots to change, you may find this tip helpful: where you want an opening quotation mark, type two little-used keyboard characters such as \\ and where you want a closing one, put ##. Copy the opening curved quotation mark from the menu, paste it into your search and replace facility and then replace the \\ characters with it. Repeat for the closing quotation mark.

1.3. Pauses and asides

Writers use various punctuation marks to indicate that the reader should pause in order to make sense of what follows. These range, in increasing length of pause, from commas, semicolons, colons and dashes to full stops.

The difference in pause between a colon and a dash is slight enough to make them interchangeable. This is worth remembering when, for layout purposes, you want to shorten the length of a line by a small amount.

Writers use pairs of commas, dashes and brackets (also known as parentheses) to tuck 'asides', which are semi-related comments or explanations, into the text. As I just did, twice.

The punctuation around an aside should relate to how closely the comment is connected to the rest of the text. Commas imply a close connection, dashes less of a connection and round brackets the least connection. In each case the aside could be omitted and the sentence would be complete.

Small points about brackets

If a punctuation mark such as a comma, full stop, exclamation mark or question mark would have occurred immediately after a word that comes before brackets, the mark is moved to follow the closing bracket. Look after the date in the first example.

When a sentence finishes with a bracket, remember that the stop or mark goes after it unless the material within the brackets is a whole sentence. (Check where the capital letter is.)

Square brackets [ ] and braces { } have special uses in mathematical notation. However, square brackets have several uses in normal documents, but should not be used when round brackets would do.

In the first example, square brackets act as sub-brackets.

In the second and third examples, square brackets are used to indicate that an explanation or comment is not part of an original text and has been inserted by the author or editor. If the comment belonged to the original, it would have been in round brackets.

('Sic' in the third example is Latin for 'thus' or 'so' and is used, usually in quotations, to indicate that an error is not the author's. It goes immediately after the word or phrase in question and can be set in italics or not.)

Colons and dashes

The first biro pens were a secret aid to the Allies' war effort — RAF crews used them for navigational calculations.

The first biro pens were a secret aid to the Allies' war effort: RAF crews used them for navigational calculations.

Square brackets

The first biro pens (invented by Laszio Biro [1900 – 1985], Hungarian painter, sculptor and journalist) were a secret aid to the Allies' war effort. RAF crews used them for navigational calculations as they did not leak with changes of altitude.

The aged knight, being ruthful [compassionate], gave her food and money.

A tenant wrote to his landlord saying, 'I was trying to mend the flush when the toilet seat broak *[sic]* in half. Will you come and fix it soon because my wife has not been able to go for three days?'

Big points about dashes

Hyphens are not dashes. When we use a typewriter we must use a hyphen to represent a dash because that is all we have. Nothing makes a document look more unprofessional than a hyphen used as a dash. Old fashioned typing practice, recognising that they were not the same things, sometimes used two hyphens to represent a dash.

When hyphens and dashes are seen together it is immediately obvious how weak a hyphen looks. Using the correct dash is one of those little details that are infallible indications of whether or not someone knows — and cares about — what they are doing when it comes to making a good impression. Hyphens have several uses that are covered later.

Time mends a broken heart - maybe.
Time mends a broken heart -- maybe.
Time mends a broken heart — maybe.

Getting into the detail of dashes, there are two kinds: em dashes, which are long, and en dashes which are shorter than em dashes, but longer than hyphens. This example shows the differences.

Hyphen	-
En dash	–
Em dash	—

As their names imply, an en dash is approximately the width of a capital N and an em dash approximately the width of a capital M.

Em dashes are used for grammatical purposes, such as for pauses and asides, as in the examples opposite.

En dashes are most often used to replace the word 'to' when linking numbers or words, and for minus signs.

As you have probably already worked out, you produce these non-keyboard dashes in the same way that you previously accessed real quotation marks. In most Windows programs an em dash is Alt+0151 and an en dash Alt+0150. In WordPerfect they are Ctrl-v 4,34 and Ctrl-v 4,33 respectively.

Let's consider whether or not to leave spaces either side of dashes: hyphens have no spaces each side and traditionally, neither do dashes. However, this practice has changed during the past quarter century. For examples, look at a book printed before the seventies and compare it with a recent book or magazine. Putting spaces either side of dashes is the practice I have adopted for this book. Neither is wrong: just be consistent.

Use of em dashes

For the first time Sue realised how exhilarating love could be — and how painful!

For the first time Ken realised — oh, the pain! — how illogical love could be.

Use of en dashes

This car does 0 – 60 mph in six seconds.

10.30 – 12.00

She caught the London – Paris express.

We open Monday – Friday.

The temperature was –5°C.

etc., e.g. and i.e.

These introduce special asides. There are two aspects to consider: when to use these Latin abbreviations, and their associated punctuation.

etc.

'etc.' is short for 'et cetera' and means 'and other things', 'and so on' or 'and so forth'. Because of its meaning, it should not be used when a list is headed by phrases like 'for example', 'e.g.', 'including' or 'such as'. It is best kept for informal or technical writing, otherwise use one of the English phrases.

'etc.' ends a list and is preceded by a comma. If embedded in a sentence it retains the full stop and is followed by the appropriate punctuation mark. If it ends the sentence, do not add another stop!

e.g. and i.e.

'e.g.' is the abbreviation of 'exempli gratia'. This means 'a gratuitous example', or usually, 'for example'. 'i.e.' stands for 'id est', which means 'that is'. The first is used before examples of something already mentioned and the latter introduces an elaboration or explanation.

The abbreviations 'e.g.' and 'i.e.' are best kept for either official or informal documents. In most cases the English phrases 'for example' and 'that is' are better style and, although 'e.g.' and 'i.e.' should never start a sentence, the English equivalents can.

Note the punctuation: the full stops are always retained and there is no space after the first stop. Unlike 'etc.' they are not followed by other punctuation marks such as a comma or colon.

What to do now

Search your document for brackets. Check whether they have been used appropriately and check the associated punctuation.

Make a pass of the document for hyphens to replace with em dashes and another for the en dashes. If hyphens with spaces each side have been used to represent em and en dashes, you can use a 'space hyphen space' sequence in your search and replace facility to look for those hyphens only, as hyphenated words will then be ignored.

Search your document for 'etc.', 'e.g.' and 'i.e.' and make any changes to wording or punctuation that are needed.

Use/avoidance of 'etc.'

All sorts of garden birds will be attracted to your bird table; sparrows, blackbirds, starlings, finches, etc.

All sorts of garden birds will be attracted to your bird table, including sparrows, blackbirds, starlings and finches.

All sorts of garden birds — sparrows, blackbirds, starlings, finches, etc. — will be attracted to your bird table whatever food you put out.

Use/avoidance of 'e.g.' and 'i.e.'

Birds which are less common in gardens, e.g. woodpeckers, wagtails and herons, may be attracted if you can set up the right conditions.

A binocular with good handling qualities, i.e. a convenient weight and size, may be more useful than one with high magnification.

A binocular with good handling qualities, that is, a convenient weight and size, may be more useful than one with high magnification.

1.4. Numbers in the body of the text

Words or numerals?

There is a convention that numbers in the body of text from one to ten (some people prefer twenty) are written out; the rest are put as numerals in most circumstances. The underlying principle is to help the eye flow along without confusing the brain. Words for large numbers start to become burdensome. The examples opposite illustrate this point and are commented on below.

1. When compared with the written number, the '3' in the example stands out unnecessarily.
2. Words for the numbers are unnecessarily long: the numerals are more easy to take in.
3. and 4. The above conventions apply to *whole* numbers. Treat decimals and ratios as large numbers.
5. and 6. If the number starts a sentence, however, write it in full if possible. To avoid writing numbers out inappropriately, re-write a sentence to put large, or decimal, numbers further into the middle.
7. Do not mix text and numerals for number ranges.

Note:
- Fractions and the numbers in the range 21 – 99 are hyphenated when written out.
- Unlike the numbers 10,000 and above, the numbers 1000 – 9999 do not, by convention, have a comma separating the thousands from the hundreds.

Percentages

The term 'per cent' is usually two words in British English and a single word in American English. 'Percentage' is one word.

8. Occasional percentages reported in text follow the same general principles as whole numbers.
9. In text with lots of percentages, use figures for all the numbers, not just those below eleven, and use the per cent symbol (%), otherwise the text would become overburdened.
10. If the whole document had only a few references to percentages, I would tend not to use the per cent symbol even with numerals.
11. The symbol is never used to stand for 'per cent' or 'percentage' by itself, or after a written number.

Do you remember the message at the very beginning of the *Quick Bits* section? Be consistent throughout the document.

Wrong	Right
1. The lorry, weighing nearly 3 tonnes, seemed to pause before toppling over the cliff edge.	The lorry, weighing nearly three tonnes, seemed to pause before toppling over the cliff edge.
2. The unladen lorry weighed two thousand, nine hundred and fifty-two kilograms.	The unladen lorry weighed 2952 kilograms.
3. The unladen lorry weighed two point nine tonnes.	The unladen lorry weighed 2.9 tonnes.
4. Cancer surgery was performed at hospitals A and B at a ratio of three to two.	Cancer surgery was performed at hospitals A and B at a ratio of 3:2.
5. 3-tonne lorries should not be parked on the edge of cliffs.	Three-tonne lorries should not be parked on the edge of cliffs.
6. 121 interviewees thought that the margarine was too soft.	The margarine was thought too soft by 121 of the interviewees.
7. Approximately eight – 12 people were trapped.	Approximately 8 – 12 people were trapped. Or: Approximately eight to twelve people were trapped.
8. Growth will be about 2%. Growth is two point two per cent. Growth is expected to be about 2 percentage points.	Growth will be about two per cent. Growth is 2.2%. Growth is expected to be about two percentage points.
9. Before the election the socialists' seven per cent lead was successively cut to six per cent, four per cent, and three per cent the day before. They won with a comfortable 14 per cent.	Before the election the socialists' 7% lead was successively cut to 6%, 4%, and 3% the day before. They won with a comfortable 14%.
10. ...only 70% of people...	...only 70 per cent of people...
11. How do you work out the % of his share? How do you work out seven %?	How do you work out the percentage of his share? How do you work out seven per cent?

Dates

The representation of dates varies according to the fashion and convention in different countries. Current practice in Britain is to use cardinal numbers (1, 2, 3, etc.) not ordinal ones (1st, 2nd, 3rd, etc.) with dates. What used to be 13th March is now usually 13 March. If you want to communicate an old-fashioned image then use the old form. Definitely do not use it if you want to create the impression of a modern, up-to-date, dynamic organisation. To some people the modern form looks rather bleak, so the fashion may change again.

More significant in terms of giving a document a professional look is the treatment of year ranges and financial years. Opposite, Example 1 is illogical as a slash usually implies alternatives rather than ranges. Example 2 looks rather tombstone-like, Example 3 looks somewhat weak, but Example 4 is a good compromise and will bear repetition in text. This format is essential for clarity when the years are in different decades, as in Example 5.

However, when the years straddle a century, the full format is essential to avoid any confusion. For example, 1463 – 1529 is clear, whereas if you tried to write it as 1463 – 29, a reader would be confused as to what it meant. With the turn of a century the full form is even more necessary: 1999 – 00 implies that '19' is omitted, giving the range 1999 – 1900.

For financial years (or other fixed twelve-month periods which are a single entity covering parts of two calendar years) the convention of using a slash rather than an en dash is best: in that way you can have financial year *ranges*. (Examples 6 and 7.) While we are on the subject of dates, BC (before Christ) goes *after* the year and AD (anno domini) goes *before*. (Example 8.)

a.m./p.m. and time formats

Despite the practice of dropping full stops from abbreviations these days, a.m. (*ante meridiem*) and p.m. (*post meridiem*) still tend to retain them to distinguish 'a.m.' from the word 'am', but it is not obligatory. There is always a space after the numbers.

In Britain, the use of capitals for time abbreviations is old-fashioned. The capitalised abbreviation stands for 'amplitude modulation' (a radio term contrasting with FM, which is 'frequency modulation') or *anno mundi* (Latin, meaning 'in the year of the world'). PM is used for 'Prime Minister' and *post-mortem*. In the USA, 'a.m.' and 'p.m.' are more commonly capitalised, in which case small caps should be used. (Small caps are explained later.)

When indicating time using a twelve hour clock, it is best to retain the a.m. and p.m. after the numbers. Writing a time as 2:45 makes it look like a ratio and is ambiguous. When using a twenty-four hour clock, all four numbers are used: there is no full stop marking the difference between the hours and minutes and the figures are followed by 'hours', not 'a.m.' or 'p.m.'.

Date ranges

1. Wine quality in the years 1982/7 was excellent.

2. Wine quality in the years 1982 – 1987 was excellent.

3. Wine quality in the years 1982 – 7 was excellent.

4. Wine quality in the years 1982 – 84 was excellent but declined in 1985 – 87 and improved again in 1988 – 98.

5. Wine quality in the years 1987 – 91 was excellent.

Financial years

6. In 1985/86, the company broke even for the first time.

7. In the financial years 1986/87 – 1993/94 our profits held steady.

BC and AD

8. He was born in 1 BC, and — there being no 'year zero' — died one year later, in AD 1.

Twelve hour clock time formats

Meet us at 1.30 a.m. in the club.
Or;
Meet us at 1.30 am in the club.
But not;
Meet us at 1.30 A.M. in the club.

Twenty-four hour clock time formats

'0630 hours' is pronounced as 'oh six thirty hours', '1352 hours' as 'thirteen fifty-two hours' and '1300 hours' as 'thirteen hundred hours'.

Fractions

Most character sets have some fractions built in and you access them as you do other non-keyboard characters. This means that you can have properly designed and proportioned ½, ¼ and ¾ symbols.

You will probably need to create more unusual fractions with a superscript number, a slash and some subscript numbers if your word processor can produce these. This is less satisfactory than using properly designed ones, but much better than just putting down ordinary sized numbers. It is better still if you reduce the size of the super- and subscripts to about eighty per cent of the rest of the text, to 10 points, for example, if you are using 12 point text generally.

In the examples on the opposite page I have put the number '7' in front of the fractions so that you can compare their sizes.

Punctuating decimals and thousands

Few people have problems punctuating decimals, but it is worth noting, for documents which may be sent abroad, that on continental Europe, commas and points are used in opposite circumstances to the way they are in Britain. To reduce this confusion, some people now just leave a space instead of a point or comma to mark thousands above 9999.

Zeros in postcodes

A small point to finish this section about numbers. Remember that the letter 'O' does not look the same as the number '0'. You sometimes see it in postcodes by mistake. I have even seen it on House of Commons headed paper, as in: SW1A OAA!

What to do now

You are now ready to search your document for numbers, percentages, dates, times and fractions to change them to an appropriate format where necessary.

It is probably easiest to scan the printed version to locate them.

Fractions

Proper characters (normal point size)	Ordinary sized numbers	Superscript/subscript (normal point size)	Superscript/subscript (reduced point size)
7¼	7 1/4	$7^1/_4$	$7^1/_4$
7½	7 1/2	$7^1/_2$	$7^1/_2$
7¾	7 3/4	$7^3/_4$	$7^3/_4$
–	7 16/22	$7^{16}/_{22}$	$7^{16}/_{22}$
–	7 2/1000	$7^2/_{1000}$	$7^2/_{1000}$

Decimal formats

British/American	European	'New'
15,473	15.473	15 473
15,473.88	15.473,88	15 473.88
2.8	2,8	2.8
1,000,000	1.000.000	1 000 000

1.5. Capitals

Our capital letters came from the letters that the Romans used, with mostly straight lines, which were fine for carving into stone, but which were very slow when writing by hand on other materials. Over time, quicker-to-write, smaller letters evolved. By the end of the eighth century these had become consolidated into what we now call 'lower case' letters.

We attach importance to capital letters: think of warning signs and their use at the beginning of the names and of sentences. There are several possible explanations why we do this. 'Bigger' generally tends to equate with 'more important', or perhaps it is a 'cultural memory' from the time when these were the only letter forms.

What, therefore, would be more natural than to put all important words into capitals? And yet the very first thing you learned to do in this book was to put words that need emphasis into italics or bold type. The sense that capitals are important lies at much of the confusion around their use in modern documents where their *visual* impact should be the prime concern.

So, visually, what do capitals do? Simply, capitals make reading harder because they are less legible than lower case letters. To look at it another way, we have to read words in capitals more slowly in order to get the meaning from them.

Why? Once we have learned to read, our eyes scan a line of text picking out word shapes rather than reading individual letters. Capitals are less varied in their shapes than lower case letters. Therefore the shape of words written in capitals is also less varied and the brain has to go more slowly to recognise the words. Reading slows down and the possibility of error increases.

The examples opposite make the point.

Small capitals

Most word processors can turn lower case letters into 'small capitals' or 'small caps' which have the shape of upper case letters but are approximately only as tall as a lower case letter 'x'. Compare the height of the small caps with the normal capitals in the examples opposite. The use of small caps is fairly limited to contexts such as dates, abbreviations and the rendering of capitals in text.

Proper small caps are not just shrunk down versions of full size capitals (which will do at a pinch), but have their proportions changed to take account of the visual effect of reducing them. They are a sophisticated touch, which should appeal to readers of this book, but should be used sparingly. Refer to your manual to find out how to produce them.

MARVELLOUS AS WAS THE PANORAMA, WE COULD NOT LONG REMAIN TO ENJOY IT, FOR WE NATURALLY WISHED TO ACCOMPLISH THE MOST DIFFICULT PART OF THE JOURNEY BEFORE NIGHTFALL. MOUNTING OUR MULES, WE SET OFF HOMEWARDS, BUT NIGHT OVERTOOK US SOON AFTER PASSING THE WATERFALL.

Marvellous as was the panorama, we could not long remain to enjoy it, for we naturally wished to accomplish the most difficult part of the journey before nightfall. Mounting our mules, we set off homewards, but night overtook us soon after passing the waterfall.

Small caps

He was born in 1 BC and died in AD 1.

The White House is in Washington DC.

On the gate was a sign which read BEWARE OF THE DOG.

Common misuses of capitals

Most people do not have problems with the normal uses of capitals: to start sentences, for proper names, and so on, but there are some traps into which we have all fallen at times. I have set out some of the most common opposite, with the explanations below.

1. Emphasis. See the earlier section on emphasis.
2. Blocks of text in all capitals. Often seen on leaflets and overhead projector slides in the belief that capitals draw more attention to themselves, which they might do, but negatively.
3. Job titles, occupations, names of departments, institutions, etc. Job titles, names of professions, names of departments and institutions are *only* capitalised if the occurrence refers to something or someone specific, or if the specific title has been abbreviated.

Beware! Inconsistent capitalisation in the above circumstances will give away which professions or occupations you regard as important.

I went to the seminar for Dental Surgeons and my husband went to the car mechanics' lecture.

I went to the seminar for dental surgeons and my husband went to the car mechanics' lecture.

There are a few exceptions. For example, 'Act' as in 'Acts of Parliament' always, by convention, has a capital 'A' regardless of where it occurs.

4. Headings and headlines. The desire to put headings and headlines into capitals comes from the sense that these are important. However, using only capitals should be avoided because, as explained above, such words are less easy to read. In the examples where capitals are used at the beginning of every word, they 'hold up' the eye as it scans the line and draw undue attention to the minor, linking words. Where the key words are capitalised and the minor ones not, this is an accepted convention — a compromise between 'importance' and 'readability'.
    One of the 'lorry' headlines implies that the lorry ran over a certain famous singer.

What to do now

Search your document to make appropriate changes to capitals in job titles, names of departments and headings. As your find facility will pick up all the capitals at the beginning of sentences, the easiest way to identify those that need changing is by looking through the version you first printed.

Wrong	Right
1. *RESIST* the *TEMPTATION* to put all important words into CAPITALS.	*Resist* the temptation to put all important words into capitals.
2. DO NOT USE ALL CAPITALS. SEE THE EXAMPLE TWO PAGES BACK.	Do not use all capitals. See the example two pages back.
3. Have you seen a Consultant Orthopaedic Surgeon do a hip replacement?	Have you seen a consultant orthopaedic surgeon do a hip replacement?
Send our leaflet to the Sales Managers and Chief Executives of the companies on the following list.	Send our leaflet to the sales managers and chief executives of the companies on the following list.
I went to watch Miss Brown, consultant orthopaedic surgeon, replace a hip.	I went to watch Miss Brown, Consultant Orthopaedic Surgeon, replace a hip.
Miss Brown is an excellent Consultant Orthopaedic Surgeon.	Miss Brown is an excellent consultant orthopaedic surgeon.
Oxford and Cambridge are University towns.	Oxford and Cambridge are university towns.
He went from Oxford to Cambridge university.	He went from Oxford to Cambridge University.
Send this memo to everyone in sales. (Implies to all sales professionals in the country. If that is so, it would be right.)	Send this memo to everyone in Sales. ('Sales' is short for *Briarwood 1000's Sales Department.*)
4. CHAPTER 1. A SHOT IN THE DARK	
Chapter 1. A Shot In The Dark (Note: 'in' and 't̲he')	Chapter 1. A Shot in the Dark
LORRY RUNS OVER CLIFF	
Lorry runs over Cliff	Lorry runs over cliff

1.6. Underlining

We have seen that for emphasis we use italic or bold text and, to draw attention to particular words without emphasising them, we use quotation marks. So what place does underlining (which is so useful in handwriting and typing) have on the printed page? The answer is *very little*.

Do not use underlining for decoration because it cuts through the descenders of the letters. If you do want to place a line under words, you need to go to the trouble of putting in a proper ruled line (or simply, a 'rule') that clears the bottom of the descenders. The first example opposite is underlined, the second has a proper rule. To create a rule, see if your word processor allows you to insert lines that you can position anywhere on the page. You are unlikely to be able to do this if you are using non Windows-based software. If you cannot insert a proper rule on a page, it may be possible to put the text into the box of a table and switch on a border for only the bottom line of the box. Rules are useful in headers and footers, more of which later.

Underlining *can* be used in some very special contexts. For example, when you wish to draw attention to part of a word, as I did in one of the examples on the misuse of capitals.

What to do now

Remove underlining from *everywhere* in your document unless if you have some of these exceptional circumstances.

1.7. Omissions from text

There are two kinds of omissions, for which an ellipsis mark (...) is used. The first type represents a lead into, or a trailing out of, a sentence. In this instance the focus of the speaker or author is being changed without being explained, as in the first and second examples opposite. The second occurs at the beginning, middle or end of a quotation, to abbreviate the text, as in the third and fourth examples. In the fourth example, the omission is from the end of the sentence. In this circumstance the final full stop is retained. *This is the only time that the ellipsis appears to be more than three stops.*

One does not put a space between an ellipsis mark and the neighbouring letters. In most fonts there is a proper character for ellipsis, which is not the same as three full stops: the inter-dot spacing is different. Here, the ellipsis is first, followed by three normal stops: ... ...

What to do now

The ellipsis symbol will be found in the character set. I am sure you know what to do to your document now...

Underpinning the
Leaning Tower of
Pisa was very difficult.

Underpinning the
Leaning Tower of
Pisa was very difficult.

Allowable use of underlining

It is important to get the stress in a word right: 'entrance' being
the way in and 'entrance' being to put someone under a spell.

Ellipsis

...And finally, winter arrived. Elizabeth put her plan into action.

Martin shouted, *Wow! Look at that go...*

He wrote, *This car...will not be beaten for value.*

He wrote, *The model made by Ford in Michigan, has
sixteen valves....*

1.8. Headings

Headings have two functions: they divide paragraphs into related chunks, helping readers locate parts of the document they are interested in, and they *should* enhance the look of pages.

Headings are actually a big subject and I will come back to them in later sections. For now, we will consider the basics.

Headings mark sections and sub-sections of documents, particularly reports. Not counting the main title of a document as a heading, four levels are usually enough:

- Sections. (First level headings.)
- Sub-sections. (Second level headings.)
- Sub-sub-sections. (Third level headings.)
- Sub-sub-sub-sections. (Fourth level headings.)

If you need more, the structure of the document has probably developed to be so cumbersome with sub-sections of sub-sub-sections that the reader is likely to become lost. Try to restructure it.

The relative importance of the headings should be indicated by variations of three elements: the point size, the weight of the text (that is, bold or not) and the font used.

We will explore the use of different fonts in headings later.

What to do now

Go through your document and decide to which level each heading belongs and change it where necessary, removing underlining, changing italics back to normal text and using capitals on appropriate main words only.

Make the difference between the levels of heading. Follow the scheme in the example opposite for now.

Level	Description	Example
Level 1 headings	Bold, 9 point sizes larger than the normal text, in this case at 20 point.	# 1. Tuning your Banjo
Level 2 headings	Bold, 5 point sizes larger than the normal. text, i.e. at 16 point.	## 1.1. The Strings in Turn
Level 3 headings	Bold, 3 point sizes larger than the normal. text, i.e. at 14 point.	### 1.1.1. How to Read Tablature
Level 4 headings	Bold normal text.	**1.1.1.1. A Basic Strum**
Normal text	11 point.	Normal text

1.9. Spaces after punctuation

I have kept this topic until we are near the end of *Quick Bits* because it makes some typists feel very uncomfortable. If you have stayed with me so far, you will trust me when I tell you that printed material, which you are trying to emulate when you create an impressive document, does not have double spaces after full stops.

Yes, it is true — pick up a book or a leaflet that has been professionally typeset and inspect the spaces after full stops. Some spaces may be stretched a little if the text is justified to both margins, but otherwise they will be only one space width, as in this text. Double spaces are a legacy of the typewriter age, when all letters and spaces were forced to be the same width and it was useful to mark the sentence boundary with the extra space. It made *typed* text easier to read, but slows down the eye as it scans *printed* text.

Perhaps some more explanation is needed. In traditional printing, like handwriting, letters and punctuation marks have different widths: the letter 'm' is wider than 'j', for example. Except for some fonts which retain the fixed typewriter spacing, like *Courier*, the fonts used by your word processor are proportionally spaced. With proportional spacing, the shape of the space over the stop and before the following capital is sufficient to help the brain spot each end of the sentence, which is all it needs to do.

There is more on the subject of letter widths and the intricacies of the space between letters later, but the principle to remember is that space should be used to help the eye and brain move swiftly and smoothly along. Unnecessary spaces are like potholes that trip up the eyes as they scan the lines — so fill them in! Compare the examples opposite.

What to do now

What can you do about putting single spaces after full stops? Could you break the habit of a typing lifetime and only type one space after a stop? Most people find that very difficult, so they carry on typing two and regularly use the search and replace facility to *automatically* change all double spaces into single ones. Do it now on your experimental document.

This procedure is worth carrying out even if you habitually only type one space. It picks up any double spaces between words that may have crept in accidentally.

Do not forget that three or more spaces will sometimes inadvertently appear in your documents and that a single search will only turn four spaces into three, or three into two. It may be necessary to run the replacement routine several times until it cannot find any more double spaces.

A final point. If you have used multiple spaces to try to align things like numbers in tables, doing this will wreck those alignments. Leave them for now. You will learn much better ways of aligning numbers in the section on tables.

Two spaces after stops

Heat hazed. Dogs dozed in doorways. Cats cooled in courtyards. Only lizards leapt into life as the man from Málaga moved slowly past. He suffered. Stopped. Swayed. Staggered. Swore in English for me to hear. *Blasta nuisance!* He knew I had heard. Unable to move I did not react.   Heat and thirst split my mind and body. Wicked words wove the scene. Unbidden, they twisted and tumbled each other: concoctions of compulsive alliteration stealing my senses.

One space after stops

Heat hazed. Dogs dozed in doorways. Cats cooled in courtyards. Only lizards leapt into life as the man from Málaga moved slowly past. He suffered. Stopped. Swayed. Staggered. Swore in English for me to hear. *Blasta nuisance!* He knew I had heard. Unable to move I did not react. Heat and thirst split my mind and body. Wicked words wove the scene. Unbidden, they twisted and tumbled each other: concoctions of compulsive alliteration stealing my senses.

1.10. Completing the makeover

Later sections deal with some matters that affect the very structure of your documents, like the subtleties of text and space. I like to think of the changes you have made so far as a 'makeover' for your document. Do not think of them as superficial, however. They must never be neglected if you want your documents to be impressive.

Before you reprint your experimental document, there are a few small topics to which it is worth paying attention and which did not find a home anywhere in the preceding sections.

Apostrophes

I see so many documents let down by failing to get apostrophes right that I think it is worth having a checklist of where to use them.

Apostrophes to indicate possession

1. Regular singular possessives: *'s* is added.

    This is the girl's room.

2. Regular plural possessives ending in *s*: Just an apostrophe is added.

    This is the girls' room.

3. Irregular plural possessives: Plurals not ending in *s* are treated in the same way as singular nouns, by adding *'s*.

    This is the women's room.
    The geese's beaks are sharp.

4. Multiple possessives: Only the last item in the list takes the apostrophe, in the appropriate place. If you feel uncomfortable with this, the sentence can usually be rewritten, as in: 'The views of the professionals and the clients differed.'

    It was Mary and Harry's house.
    The professionals and the clients' views differed.

5. Names and words ending in *s, z or x*, that are *one syllable* in length: The addition of *'s* is usually preferred.

    James's pencil.
    The fox's den.

6. Names of *more* than one syllable ending in *s, z or x*: Usually, only an apostrophe is added. However, for other words, usage is less fixed.

    It was Dickens' first work.
    A princess' secretary. *Or:* A princess's secretary.

7. Possessive pronouns: Personal possessive pronouns (including *its*) do not take an apostrophe, but indefinite pronouns do.

    It is his book.
    Give the book its full title.
    Is it anyone's book?

8. Commercial organisations: Modern practice is to omit the apostrophe (despite Sainsbury's logo).

    Find it at W H Smiths. (*Not:* Smith's)

9. One to watch: The apostrophe is often missed with units of time, which should be treated like any other words.

    It was only a minute's wait.
    He did five years' hard labour. (i.e. He did five years of hard labour.)

Apostrophes to indicate omissions

10. To indicate missing letters or numbers: Apostrophes are used to represent missing letters. The tail always points to the left.

    Four o'clock in the mornin'.
    Who's that lady?
    Rock 'n' Roll. (*Not:* Rock 'n' Roll)
    What's 'e got in 'is bag, then?

11. One to watch: *It's* means *it is*. The possessive *its* does not have an apostrophe, remember?

    It's in the bag.

12. Shortened forms of words: It is no longer necessary to use an apostrophe to indicate an omission where the shortened form of the word is in common use.

    Find it in the phone directory.
    (*Not:* Find it in the 'phone directory.)

13. Dates: The first example refers to the decade because the apostrophe represents the missing date numbers. The second means that the temperature was between 20 and 29 degrees. In both cases the *s* marks the plural and is not a possessive or an omission, and so there is no apostrophe before either.

    It was in the '20s.
    It was in the 20s.

Apostrophes and plurals

14. Plural abbreviations: It used to be correct to indicate a plural abbreviation by inserting an apostrophe before the *s*. This practice is now out of favour. An apostrophe only makes an appearance if the abbreviation is a possessive, when normal rules about its placement apply. This maintains the logical distinction between the plurals in the first example and the possessives in the second and third.

    MPs, like GPs, hold surgeries.
    Here is the GP's surgery.
    Here are the GPs' surgeries.

15. Like all good rules, there is an exception to the above! That is, for the plurals of single letters and numbers.

    The x's mark the place to sign.
    He writes his 9's in an odd way.
    (*But:* He writes his 'nines' in an odd way.)

16. Uneducated plurals: People reveal something about themselves when they put apostrophes into ordinary plurals.

    Tomatoes 80p a kilo. (*Not:* Tomato's)
    We visited the chateaux. (*Not:* chateaux's)
    Mike's Autos (*Not:* Auto's)

Two final points on apostrophes:

- If you are ever still unsure whether or not there should be one, remember the saying *If in doubt, leave it out!* A missing apostrophe is less irritating to readers than a misplaced one.
- Apostrophes are the same character as the ending quotation mark. Use the curved one, not the straight quotation mark.

Hyphenated word combinations

Hyphens are used to separate prefixes from words when, without them, the word created would look so odd that it might interrupt the reader's flow.

Re-engineer. *Not* reengineer.
De-ice. *Not* deice.
Anti-itch. *Not* antiitch.

Apart from that, hyphens are used to form compound words. Some compound forms should be hyphenated and some not.

Compounds where the second part ends in '-ed' are usually hyphenated. The numbers 21 to 99 when written in full, fractions and three word combinations always are.

A primary care-led NHS.
Seventy-nine and three-quarters.
Meet my daughter-in-law.
A five-year-old child. (*But note:* Paul was five years old.)

Compounds where an adjective is intensified by a word ending in '-ly' are never hyphenated.

She was a highly courageous woman.
Wear a brightly coloured hat.

Be aware that in other cases of compound words the practice is changing, with the tendency being to omit the hyphen and either run the words together or leave a space.

She was a high-flyer.
She was a highflyer.
She was a high-flying executive.
She was a high flying executive.

Sometimes a hyphen must be used to avoid ambiguity. In this example the hyphen makes it clear which is mashed.

Oh! Mashed potato omelettes!
Oh! Mashed-potato omelettes!

A hyphen is retained to make the meaning clear when the second word in a repeated combination is dropped to avoid duplication.

My shirts are small-sized or medium-sized.
My shirts are small- or medium-sized.

The principle to apply if you are in doubt about whether or not to put in a hyphen is: *Leave it out unless the meaning is otherwise unclear.*

Acronyms

Acronyms, that is words made up from initials, are usually represented in text in all capitals (not small caps), without punctuation marks.

Quango (Quasi-Autonomous Non-Governmental Organisation) is a case where an acronym has become so widely used as a noun to describe semi-public bodies supported by governmental funding that it has become a word in its own right. (Note that the plural of 'quango' is 'quangos', without an 'e'.)

Ampersand (&)

Only ever use an ampersand in company names and abbreviations: never to replace 'and' in continuous text or headings.

Send for a Sears & Roebuck catalogue.
They invested heavily in R&D.
Cattle Rearing and You.
Not: Cattle Rearing & You.

Principal principles

Management reports often discuss principles, that is, rules that underlie attitudes or actions. They also often talk about the principal (that is, main) features or benefits of products or courses of action. The problem is that when authors of such reports confuse the spellings, it sows the seed of doubt that they really understand their subject. The simple test is whether the word 'main' can be substituted and the sentence still retain the same kind of meaning. If it can, the spelling should be '-al', and if not, '-le'. Now you can sort them out.

There are lots of words that are similar but have distinct meanings and to clarify them, I enthusiastically recommend *The Good Word Guide* (details of which are in Part 8. *Going Further*). It is a book to which I turn more frequently than my dictionary. It pilots you through many potential hazards of spelling, pronunciation, grammar, punctuation, word usage and 'buzz words'.

and/or

The combination 'and/or' is all right to use in official or commercial documents to denote three possibilities, when the construction '...or...or both' would otherwise need to be used.

You must write a book and/or an article.
You must write a book or an article or both.

Do not use it where just 'or' or 'and' are sufficient.

You must write a book or an article.
You must write a book and article.

What to do now

You are ready to complete the makeover of your document by seeking out and changing where necessary:

- Apostrophes.
- Hyphenated word combinations.
- Acronyms.
- Ampersands.
- Principles and principals.
- 'and/or' constructions.

1.11. Checklist

You are nearly ready to print your revamped document so that you can compare it with the old.

Before you do, use the checklist opposite to make sure that you have covered everything.

Finally, run a spell check. This is always good practice last thing before printing. If there are some words that you know you regularly mistype and which form other words, so the checker will not pick them up, run separate search and replace routines for these. Two of my usual errors are 'form' for 'from' and making references to 'compliant' letters instead of 'complaint' letters!

Now print.

When you have printed

Compare your revised document with your first one. It will probably be 'crisper and cleaner' than the first, but it will not yet be an *Impressive Document*. For that we will need to start manipulating the text and the layout. These are the subjects of the next sections.

Part 2. Managing Text

The *Quick Bits* section dealt with detail in text: this section deals with all the advanced features of text that you will need to be familiar with in order to produce *Impressive Documents*.

2.1. Paragraph styles

This topic is fundamental to making best use of all of those that follow. This is not because you cannot undertake the changes without, but because, to make all the changes throughout a long document one-by-one would be too laborious and it would be difficult to use the find/replace facility. The style facility of most modern word processing software,[*] and all desktop publishing programs, allows you to modify — and experiment with — the look of the whole document very quickly.

A paragraph style is a description of a text format (font, size, margin settings, etc.) that is given a name. Some word processors come with pre-defined styles as well as ones that users can define. When other paragraphs are assigned the style name they then take on *all* the characteristics of the named style.

The style facility is called different things in different software, such as 'styles', 'named styles', 'style sheets', 'paragraph styles', 'tags' and 'tagged styles'.

If you do not already know how to use styles, open a new document to explore this feature before we make changes to your experimental document. Work through the instructions and examples in your word processor manual or on-screen help.

When you have done that, you should know how to:
- Identify the name of the style that applies to your current paragraph.
- Identify the characteristics that comprise the styles in your document. (Font, size, bold or not, indents, etc.)
- Rename styles.
- Change the characteristics of styles.
- Create and save new styles, transfer them from one document to another and delete them when necessary.
- Apply styles to your paragraphs by using keystrokes as well as through menus if you have them.

Now that you are familiar with the principles of named styles and how to manipulate them in your word processor, let's return to your experimental document.

---

[*] The word processors 'Write' and 'Wordpad' that come with Windows and Windows 95 do not have this facility. They are intended for producing small documents and therefore lack most of the powerful automating features that make full sized word processors so useful. With Windows-based software, you will know if you have a paragraph style facility because there will be a drop-down list on a toolbar saying something like 'normal' or 'body text'.

The style facility of most modern word processing software allows you to modify — and experiment with — the look of the whole document very quickly.

2.2. Automatic numbering

This topic almost went into *Quick Bits* because it is about saving tremendous amounts of time. The problem was that to automatically assign the right level of numbering to headings you need to know about styles. Also, until you start to incorporate automatic numbering into your documents as a matter of course, it takes a while to work through a document and make all the appropriate changes.

Numbering headings

I meet many people who never bother with the automatic numbering facility that most word processors provide. This is really surprising because it saves so much time and worry.

Let's assume that your experimental document is to be the kind where headings are numbered. Documents where paragraphs are numbered but the headings are not, are dealt with later.

What to do now

Open your document and scroll through it assigning your headings to named heading styles, for example: 'Heading 1', 'Heading 2', etc. Make sure that all the paragraphs that make up the body of the text of the document are assigned to the normal (or body text) style. You will find that the quickest way of assigning the styles is to use keystrokes rather than pulling them down from a menu.

Automatic numbering works by putting special codes into your document where you want the numbers to be. If you do not already know how to put in codes for automatic numbers, refer to your word processor manual to see how to do so and then work through your document, on screen, deleting any hand-inserted heading numbers and replacing them with automatic ones. (Hint: insert one code for doing this, copy it and then paste it in all the places where you need it. This saves a lot of effort and time fetching codes from scratch.)

Once you have told your word processor the level of each heading, it will keep track of the following sub-numbering sequence and 'know' how many digits to put into your heading for each level. What is more, it will automatically change them if you promote or demote a heading from one level to another. Remember the first example opposite from *Quick Bits*? By promoting the Heading 3 to Heading 2, and Heading 4 to 3, we would see the numbers change automatically as in the second example.

When you have gone through the document adding automatic numbering codes to your headings, move some of your sub-sections and enjoy seeing all the subsequent numbers in the document change without retyping!

Headings as in *Quick Bits*

Heading 1	**1. Tuning your Banjo**
Heading 2	**1.1. The Strings in Turn**
Heading 3	**1.1.1. How to Read Tablature**
Heading 4	**1.1.1.1. A Basic Strum**

Promoting heading 3 to 2 and heading 4 to 3

Heading 1	**1. Tuning your Banjo**
Heading 2	**1.1. The Strings in Turn**
Heading 2	**1.2. How to Read Tablature**
Heading 3	**1.2.1. A Basic Strum**

Numbering paragraphs

The automatic numbering principle works with paragraphs. Some documents have paragraphs numbered continuously from the beginning to the end, as in the first example opposite.

A variation is to have automatic numbering in section headings (and not other headings) after which the paragraphs are numbered — see the second example. The paragraph numbering will continue regardless of the sub-headings in the section. Each paragraph will then begin with the section number, which is quite useful for reference purposes.

What to do now

If you followed the above instructions, your document has numbered headings, but what if it had, or you wanted it to have, numbered paragraphs instead? You would need to replace any hand-inserted numbers with automatic number codes using the copy and paste technique described earlier. I once did this to a document I was editing with ninety paragraphs. It seemed very laborious but, in doing so, I found that the person who had typed it had skipped (or deleted) paragraph twenty-two and so all the subsequent ones were incorrectly numbered! With the automatic numbering there were no such problems when I changed them around.

What else can you automatically number?

Page numbers

Do not type page numbers — ever. For the same reasons as automatic heading and paragraph numbering, always use the automatic page numbering facility. Most word processors enable you to place the number exactly where you want it on the page.

Lists

Numbered lists are slightly different to numbered paragraphs as they may be part of such a paragraph.

Fortunately, the software codes that automatically number lists keeps them separate from headings or paragraphs so the two do not get confused. As you move items around the list they are re-numbered automatically.

2. A Basic Strum

2.1 The basic banjo strum is:
   1. The index finger of the right hand plucks the first string.
   2. The other three fingers brush down across all five strings.
   3. The thumb plucks the fifth string downwards.

'Numbered lists' may also be headed by sequences of letters or Roman numerals, according to whichever you choose. Roman numerals tend to be associated with an 'old fashioned' look, and lettered lists with complicated official documents, as in 'Section 2, Sub-section b), Paragraphs iii – xvi.'

Paragraphs numbered only

Heading 1
Tuning your Banjo

1. Use a pitch pipe or piano if you are going to play with other people.

2. If you are playing by yourself the absolute pitch does not matter too much as long as the strings are tuned to each other.

Heading 2
The Strings in Turn

3. Banjo strings are numbered 5 – 1 in sequence from the short string. The lowest note is produced by the open fourth string.

4. Most banjo players these days tune their instruments to a G chord across the open stings.

Heading 2
How to Read Tablature

5. Tablature is the traditional way of writing banjo music. Even if you cannot read traditional music notation you can figure out a tune from tablature.

6. The five tablature lines represent the banjo strings.

Heading 3
A Basic Strum

7. Holding a chord with your left hand, the basic banjo strum begins with the index finger of the right hand plucking the first string.

8. The other three fingers brush down across all five strings, immediately followed by the thumb plucking the fifth string with a downward motion.

Sections and paragraphs numbered

Heading 1
1. Tuning your Banjo

1.1 Use a pitch pipe or piano if you are going to play with others.

Heading 2
The Strings in Turn

1.2 Banjo strings are numbered 5 – 1 in sequence from the short string. The lowest note is produced by the open fourth string.

Heading 1
2. How to Read Tablature

2.1 Tablature is the traditional way of writing banjo music. Even if you cannot read traditional music notation you can figure out a tune from tablature.

Heading 3
A Basic Strum

2.2 Holding a chord with your left hand, the basic banjo strum begins with the index finger of the right hand plucking the first string.

Anything else to automatically number?

When you get the hang of it, you may find that your word processing software allows you to automatically number all sorts of things such as cross references, footnotes, endnotes, table captions and picture captions. Great!

What to do now

Work through your document automating the numbering of any appropriate lists. If you only have bulleted lists, automatically number one of those.

Check your manual or on-screen help to find out what else you can number or reference automatically.

2.3. Tables of contents

Clever word processors define their tables of contents from the headings once you have assigned styles to them. Moreover, you only have to specify the range of headings to include in the table and you can have either a simple contents table, with only the main headings, or a more complex one, with several sets of sub-headings.

With less sophisticated word processors you have to work through the document defining which headings you want included in the table. It is still worth doing though, because once you have identified them, any changes are quick and easy to update, along with accurate identification of page numbers.

2.4. Indexes

Indexes are less commonly found in reports than in books, but it is worth remembering that the same applies to automating indexes as tables of contents, except that one usually has to work through the document identifying the first index entries as you need to be more selective and flexible than with contents.

What to do now

Set up at least an automated table of contents at the beginning of your document and experiment with setting up an index if you wish.

Concentrate on doing the task in hand as well as you can. If you are assembling or sorting out the text, do not bother about how the finished document might look.

2.5. Lists

This topic deals with managing lists, other than numbering them automatically. Let's start with two general points about lists:

1. Lists bring together, but also separate, pieces of information so that readers can absorb that information more rapidly. Lists should help, and not hinder, the readers' understanding of the contents.

2. Items in a list have a relationship to each other. The second point, therefore, is that the form of a list should reflect the relationship of its items.

Types of lists

There are three types of list:

- Bulleted.
- Continuous.
- Numbered.

There is something of a mania these days for bulleted lists, probably reflecting the fact that more people are using word processors that can produce them easily. However, when producing documents, use them sparingly: consider the other possibilities first.

Lists that have a logical sequence to them, such as a list of instructions, should be numbered in their appropriate order. It sounds obvious but, with the current fashion for lists to be bulleted, the point is sometimes forgotten. In this context it does not matter whether the list items are headed by digits, Roman numerals or letters, as long as they are consistent throughout the document. Automatic numbering of lists has been dealt with in the previous section.

Items in some lists are short and you may want the reader to continue reading smoothly. Use a continuous list comprising items separated by a colon and semicolons or commas in the text, as in this short example.

We had a choice of: angel cake; iced buns; almond slices; tarts, of all kinds; hand-made biscuits and pastries.

Save bullets for lists where the items in the list are long, or where you want to liven up the page *and when* the order of the items is not significant.

Producing a bulleted list

To produce a good-looking bulleted list, there are things to avoid, and some principles to follow:

- Do not just take a 'continuous list', break it up and put bullets in front of the lines. The semicolons or commas no longer make sense! For example:

    We had a choice of:
    * angel cake;
    * tarts, of all kinds;
    * hand-made biscuits and
    * pastries.

    Either treat each bulleted line as a separate sentence and start with a capital and finish with a full stop, or leave it more open, with no capital and no full stop. Both approaches are acceptable, but do not mix them in the same document.

    The style with capitals and full stops seems more appropriate when an item in the list has more than one sentence — as in the list you are reading — but do you want every bulleted list to conform to that style? If not, logic dictates that you will have to omit the full stop from the end of those sentences.

    At the final draft stage do a special check to make sure that the punctuation of the bulleted lists is consistent.

- Avoid using hyphens or asterisks for bullets, as was used in the example above. Stick to simple round dots, the same point size, or slightly smaller, as the font you are using. Squares, diamonds and gimmicks such as hands with pointing fingers have their place in documents such as leaflets, but are best avoided in serious reports unless you are really confident of the look you are trying to create. Whatever you use, make sure that it is the same bullet throughout. Obvious? I have seen many documents that use several different bullet styles. Usually by accident rather than design.

- Do not indent the bullets, but align them with the left margin.

- Indent the text with a modest gap **about equal to the length of an em dash** between it and the bullet. This point also applies to numbered lists. A small gap allows the eye to flow smoothly down the page and gives maximum line length.

- Always left justify the text in bulleted lines, leaving the right hand ragged, even if the rest of the text is fully justified (justified to both right and left margins). Bulleted lines are always uneven in length and they look thin and mean if they are stretched out to justify them to the right.

By grouping items of information together in a list, the author of a document can save unnecessary repetition by heading it with a general statement that applies to all the following items. The lists can be introduced by a full stop or, more commonly, a colon at the end of the preceding text. If it is a colon, do not follow it with dash (:—). This has gone out of fashion.

Even worse is a hyphen with a colon (:-).

What do you do if an item in a bulleted list itself contains a bulleted list? Either turn the sub-bulleted list into a continuous one, or set up a sub-bullet of a different character. Personally, I like the simplicity of an em dash, as in this example, but choose what *you* like.

- Main bullet item.
- Main bullet item, followed by:
  — sub-item
  — sub-item
  — sub-item
  — sub-item
- Main bullet item.

What to do now

Check your document for lists and consider the appropriate form for them, that is, bulleted, continuous or numbered. Make changes as necessary, including removing hyphens or dashes after colons.

Give your numbered list and bulleted list paragraphs style names. Incorporating the formatting — such as the bullet style, gap between bullet and text and the left justification — into the paragraph style will make changing all the list items easier. We will use that facility when improving lists further in *Managing Space*.

2.6. Managing line ends

There are few things more likely to slip past the unwary person using a word processor than what happens at the ends of lines. Most people do not give line ends a second thought, other than thinking about whether to justify the text to the right as well as the left margin. However, as you are someone who wants to start producing impressive documents, you will start to give several thoughts to the matters of justification, hyphenation, hangers-on and widows and orphans once you have worked through this section.

Justifying lines

Everyone who uses a word processor is aware that text can be justified (have its edges lined up) either on the left or right margins or both, or centred between the margins. What is not explained is the effect these different ways of presenting text have on the reader and some of the subtle things you need to do to make effective use of them.

In general, text justified to both margins still carries something of an air of authority, at least in official documents. This association probably lingers from pre-word processor days when most

There are few things more likely to slip past the unwary person using a word processor than what happens at the ends of lines.

documents were typed and only important, official documents were sent for printing. Those documents tended to come back justified to both margins, which, at the time, was only something that printers' typesetters could do easily.

Justification to both margins is therefore not appropriate to documents to which you want to give a friendly, inviting impression. For these, choose left-justified text with a ragged right margins.

To set a body of text with a right-justified margin and a ragged left one would be considered perverse by most people, although there are occasions (in advertising, for example) when it can be used to good effect. Generally the right justification facility is used in tables or to align small pieces of text, such as headers and footers, with the right margin.

Defining a style for your body text that contains the justification you want will help you keep your document looking consistent.

What to do now

Experiment with changing the justification in your normal (body text) style and see the effect on your experimental document. Print out a page in each style. Do they send out different messages?

Hyphenation

In this topic we are not dealing with hyphens in word combinations (see *Quick Bits*), but hyphens at the end of lines of text.

Normally, word processors take words that are too long to fit on the end of a line and move them to the beginning of the next. A hyphen enables the part of the word to the left of it to pop back up to the previous line. The reason you might want to split a word in this way is to reduce unsightly space. This is easy to demonstrate in this piece of text that is justified to both margins and not hyphenated. (Top example.) Look at the spaces in the third and fourth lines and the word dangling at the bottom of the paragraph.

The bottom example is the same text with just one hyphen inserted. Note how it reduces the inter-word space in the third line to more normal proportions. The hyphen also affects the following text, making it all more compact and saving a line. The narrower the column, as in a newsletter, the more noticeable large inter-word spaces are and the more important it is to hyphenate the text.

Unhyphenated text

Six is the lowest number of flasks quoted as needed, up to sixty! It became clear that a modular set-up based on multiples of three flasks would be appropriate for users' needs, allowing them to expand as business develops. The data recording regimes need to be as flexible as possible, from every minute over a few hours, to every ten minutes over a few days, to once a day over twenty-eight days.

Hyphenated text

Six is the lowest number of flasks quoted as needed, up to sixty! It became clear that a modular set-up based on multiples of three flasks would be appropriate for users' needs, allowing them to expand as business develops. The data recording regimes need to be as flexible as possible, from every minute over a few hours, to every ten minutes over a few days, to once a day over twenty-eight days.

For more examples of the effect of hyphenation, this time where the text is only justified on the left, look at 1, 2 and 3 opposite. I am using a larger text with settings more typical of a report or letter. Look at the first block of text and notice just how ragged the right hand edge looks.

Stage 2 has been hyphenated to reduce the raggedness, producing a straighter, smoother right-hand margin. However, the hyphenation is rather forced and awkward. The second line is still also rather short because I have forced 'Dr' onto the next line to keep it with 'Browning'. The approach to hyphenation has, therefore, to be sensitive.

In the third stage, the indentation on the right-hand side has been eased out by only 8.5mm (0.3 inches). *Dr Browning is* comes back onto the second line and enables the hyphenation to be reduced, but still gives the right margin a neater look. Not only that, but the whole block has been reduced by one line from ten to nine. This technique cannot be employed on text that is justified to both margins because the block would be instantly noticeable, jutting out into the right margin.

Successful hyphenation

Successful hyphenation does not draw attention to itself: the reader's eye flows smoothly along the line, the brain subconsciously anticipates the rest of the word from the first part, has its guess confirmed as the eye passes to the next line, and carries smoothly on.

Watch out for those things that disturb this automatic process and draw attention to the hyphens, such as:

- Hyphenating short words.
- Hyphenating words in the middle of a syllable.
- Putting the hyphen where split words form two separate and different words.
- Having more than two line ends hyphenated after each other. A run of hyphenated line ends is called a 'ladder'.

The final example opposite contains all these faults.

A good place to hyphenate words that contain double letters is between them, as long as doing so does not break any of the above 'rules'.

Most word processing software has the option of being able to hyphenate the whole document automatically. Although you can usually set it to avoid the worst of the above faults, by giving instructions such as 'no runs of more than two hyphenated lines' or 'do not hyphenate words of seven letters or less', automated hyphenation cannot bring the subtlety to the process that you can.

Putting in hyphens manually is one of the last tasks to do as you prepare your document for printing, after finally deciding the layout and after spell-checking, so do not do it as you go along.

Stage 1

On the matter of obtaining the appropriate hearing tests and the comment about 'deformed ear drums' that appears to have been worrying you, Dr Browning is sure that she did not use that phrase, but if she gave the impression that Gemma's ear drums were not anatomically correct, she apologises. She assures me that her ear drums appeared to be normal and it was the tympanogram result that suggested that Gemma had secretory otitis media (glue ears). The referral to Mr Williams for further investigation and an opinion is the normal course of action when there is some doubt. The tympanography machine Dr Browning was using at the time did not always give consistent results and it has been replaced.

Stage 2

On the matter of obtaining the appropriate hearing tests and the comment about 'deformed ear drums' that appears to have been worrying you, Dr Browning is sure that she did not use that phrase, but if she gave the impression that Gemma's ear drums were not anatomically correct, she apologises. She assures me that her ear drums appeared to be normal and it was the tympanogram result that suggested that Gemma had secretory otitis media (glue ears). The referral to Mr Williams for further investigation and an opinion is the normal course of action when there is some doubt. The tympanography machine that Dr Browning was using at the time did not always give consistent results and it has been replaced.

Stage 3

On the matter of obtaining the appropriate hearing tests and the comment about 'deformed ear drums' that appears to have been worrying you, Dr Browning is sure that she did not use that phrase, but if she gave the impression that Gemma's ear drums were not anatomically correct, she apologises. She assures me that her ear drums appeared to be normal and it was the tympanogram result that suggested that Gemma had secretory otitis media (glue ears). The referral to Mr Williams for further investigation and an opinion is the normal course of action when there is some doubt. The tympanography machine that Dr Browning was using at the time did not always give consistent results and it has been replaced.

Poor hyphenation

The profession of Speech and Language Therapy sits uneasily in the National Health Service as many therapists in Britain work predominantly with school and pre-school children. They find they have much more in common with teachers and educational psychologists than with people in the medical professions and they resist the notion of the children they work with as 'patients'.

What to do now

Save your experimental document. Turn on automatic hyphenation and browse through the document to see what effect it has had on your line ends. Now turn it off. The automatically inserted hyphens should disappear by themselves. If they do not, then close your document without saving and re-open the version you just saved.

Now find a reasonably long paragraph so that you can try manual hyphenation. It does not matter whether your document has body text that is justified to both margins or has a ragged right margin. Start at the top of the paragraph and look down the left-hand side of the paragraph looking for long words that have wrapped onto the beginning of lines. Insert a hyphen into such a word. The first part of the word should dart back up to the line before. If the hyphen is too far to the right, or if there is insufficient space on the line before, the word will not break. Keeping to the 'rules', about where not to hyphenate, experiment with inserting the hyphen in different places in the word.

Note the effect that each change has on the current line and all the lines below — it can sometimes be dramatic.

Manually inserted hyphens are not usually removed automatically if the words containing them are subsequently shifted into the body of the text *but* some word processors allow you to insert a third kind of hyphen (sometimes called an 'optional hyphen') that appears when the word breaks at that point and disappear if the words are moved. This is the best hyphen to use if you can.

When you have finished experimenting, remove the hyphens. You will hyphenate the document later, after deciding on a new layout.

Widows and orphans

Widows and orphans are, respectively, the first and last lines of paragraphs that become detached from the rest of the paragraph to which they belong, either on a page or in a column. This descriptive name was given by typographers because they look lonely, and besides, no one wants to make widows or orphans.

Most word processors have 'widow and orphan control'. This forces another line from the rest of the paragraph to join the widow or orphan so that it is no longer alone. It is better, if the layout or text allows, to prevent a widow by forcing a column break or page break to move the line on to join the rest, or to shorten a paragraph to reabsorb an orphan.

Widows and orphans

Widows and orphans are first and last lines of paragraphs that become detached from the rest of the paragraph to which they belong, either on a page or in a column. This descriptive name came about because they look odd and lonely and, besides, no one wants to make widows or orphans.

Most word processing

widow

programs have 'widow and orphan control'. This forces another line from the paragraph to join the widow or orphan so that it is no longer alone. It is better, if the layout or text allows, to prevent widows by forcing a column break or page break moving the line on to join the rest, or shorten a paragraph so that you can then

orphan

reabsorb an orphan.

Widows and orphans are first and last lines of paragraphs that become detached from the rest of the paragraph to which they belong, either on a page or in a column. This name came about because they look odd and lonely and besides, no one wants to make widows or orphans, do they?

Hangers-on and danglers

There are some things that should be kept together on the same line. What do you think of the first batch of examples opposite?

It is much better to keep things like dates, titles and names and some hyphenated compounds together, as in the second batch.

I call the parts of this kind of combination that become left behind 'hangers-on', because of the way that they hang on to the end of the line when the word processor moves the rest to the next line. There are four ways to prevent these kinds of combinations from breaking:

1. The most satisfactory way to prevent the break happening at a space is to use a 'non-breaking space' between the words that you want to keep together. (Non-breaking spaces may be called something else in your word processor. WordStar calls them 'binding spaces', for example.) Refer to your manual or on-screen help to find out how to insert one. The word processor will treat the 'word+non-breaking space+word' combination as a single entity and move them together, from the end of the line above, down to the next line. If you later edit the text and the combination moves into the middle of a line, it does not matter. This is how '18' and 'Dr' were moved in the examples. Exactly the same principle applies to non-breaking hyphens if you can insert them.

2. In the third example, non-breaking hyphens would have taken the whole of 'daughter-in-law' to the next line, leaving the first line very short. To avoid this I adopted the second tactic, which is to move the right-hand indentation (for that paragraph only) a fraction towards the right margin until the whole phrase moved back to the line above. (In the same way that I did in one of the hyphenation examples.) You cannot do this if your paragraphs are justified to both margins because it would disturb the line of the justification down the page.

3. The third (and least satisfactory) way to ensure that the 'hanger-on' moves to the next line is to insert a 'soft break' before it. This, if you are not familiar with the terminology, is an instruction to the word processor that tells it where the line ends so that it wraps at that point. It does not treat the line end as if it were the end of a paragraph, which, by contrast is a 'hard break' and occurs when you press the 'Return', 'Enter' or the ↵ key on your keyboard. The problem with soft breaks (look up how to put them in) is that if you edit the paragraph, or change the width of normal para-graphs using the style facility, the soft break can end up in the middle of a line
and have an odd effect. Like that.

Examples of hangers-on

He alleges that on his visit to the clinic 18 May
1971, the doctor could not find his notes.

He alleges that on his visit to the clinic 18 May the doctor he saw, Dr
Jones, could not find his notes and gave him the wrong injection.

Dr Jones said that at the clinic 18 May, the patient's daughter-
in-law, Ms Smith, was verbally abusive towards him.

Hangers-on — moved on

He alleges that on his visit to the clinic
18 May 1971, the doctor could not find his notes.

He alleges that on his visit to the clinic 18 May the doctor he saw,
Dr Jones, could not find his notes and gave him the wrong injection.

Dr Jones said that at the clinic 18 May, the patient's daughter-in-law,
Ms Smith, was verbally abusive towards him.

4. The final way to deal with hangers-on is to edit the text so that the combination you do not want to break is moved further into the line. This is fine — unless you inadvertently edit it back again later!

In general, use a non-breaking space or hyphen if you can.

There is another kind of hanger-on, which some people call an 'orphan', but this is confusing because of the use of this term in 'widows and orphans'. This kind of hanger-on is more of a 'dangler'. It is a short word (say, seven letters or less) that hangs on to the bottom of a paragraph, playing at being a line all by itself.

As you just noticed, such 'danglers' reduce the compactness and integration of a page by adding more space than is needed between the bottom of one paragraph and the next.

To get rid of danglers you either have to find a way of word-wrapping them back into the bulk of the paragraph or bring in extra words to join them on the last line, so that they are no longer alone.

- To move the word back you can:
  - Hyphenate the line ends.
  - Ease out the right indentation.
  - Turn a dash into a colon. (Remember from *Quick Bits*?)
  - Edit, reducing the number of words in the paragraph. This has the advantage that such editing usually improves the style of writing.

- To bring words onto the last line of the paragraph you can:
  - Add some words to the paragraph.
  - Unhyphenate words.
  - Spell out abbreviated words.
  - Move the right indentation to the left.
  - Force the word before the dangler to move to the last line by using a soft break or non-breaking space.

What to do now

In the version of your experimental document printed at the end of *Quick Bits*, look for widows, orphans, hangers-on and danglers. Just see if you have any, but do not do anything about them now — you will get rid of them later.

**The eye and brain are
extremely good at detecting
variations in printed text, even
when the person cannot explain
the cause of the variation.**

2.7. Legibility and subtle messages

For most purposes, the priority when producing text is to make it easy to read for its target readership. Otherwise, why bother? Certainly, busy people will not struggle to read text that is difficult to decipher. This does not mean that one only ever uses a single font (traditionally called a 'typeface' in printing[*]) which you never change. If that were so, no one would have bothered to produce so many varieties of type. There is another consideration when choosing a font: its look will 'send out' a subtle message — the visual equivalent of perfume.

This section explains the factors of font size, category and style that you need to take into consideration for legibility and also the subtle messages conveyed by different fonts. Matching a font to the purpose of your document does not take long and will enhance it enormously.

Font size and legibility

The first factor that influences how easily your target audience will read your document is the size of the type you use.

The size of printed letters is measured in 'points'. There are 72 points to an inch (25.4mm). The measure is taken from the top of the ascenders to the bottom of the descenders, as illustrated in the diagram opposite.

The size of type that is comfortable to read varies as we grow older. This is due to a combination of reading skill, mental agility and eyesight. New readers manage better with fairly large type, say, 15 or more points in children's books, but teenagers can feel quite comfortable with type as small as 9 points, as a look at their magazines will show. Adult readers get on better with type between 10 and 13 points and older people appreciate text in point sizes 13 to 14. Larger point sizes for ordinary text can be perceived as patronising, unless deliberately made large for people with visual problems, as in large-print books. Compare the examples opposite.

---

[*] The terminology of typefaces and fonts has changed. When type was made of metal, a style of print character was called a typeface. Printers needed large numbers of sets of these in different sizes. For example, they might have several sets of their favourite typefaces in different point sizes, plus more sets in italics and yet more in bold. Each set of typeface, point size and character style was called a 'font' and the number of individual pieces of type printers needed was immense. Now that typefaces are stored on computer, it is almost universal to use 'font' to describe the typeface, making reference to its size in points when necessary.

Measuring fonts

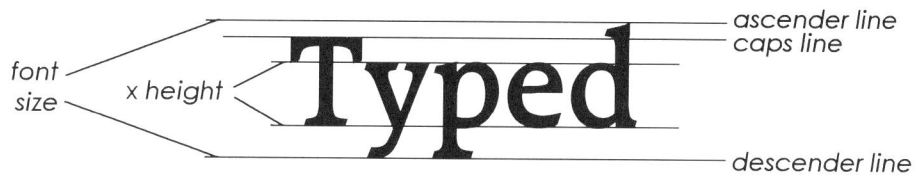

font size   x height   Typed   ascender line   caps line   descender line

Different sizes for different purposes

In the woods, the bears will eat you.   (15 point)

In the woods, the bears will eat you.   (9 point)

In the woods, the bears will eat you.   (11 point)

In the woods, the bears will eat you.   (13.5 point)

In the woods, the bears will eat you.   (18 point)

Font categories and legibility

The second consideration for legibility is the kind of font used. Fonts fall into related categories. The list opposite is not comprehensive but gives an idea of the main ones (there are eleven categories in the British Standard). All the examples of different fonts in the text are in the same point size and none are in their bold form, but you will easily see that they take up different amounts of space and some appear to be heavier or lighter than others. The choice of font therefore affects the overall appearance of a page.

Old Style fonts

Old style serif fonts have the advantage of being considerably quicker for most people to read than sans serif fonts. You may remember from the section on capitals that shape is important for rapid word recognition. With serifs, word shapes are more distinctive and the eye skims easily along the line, helped by transitions the serifs make from letter to letter.

Sans Serif fonts

Sans serif fonts can be clearer than serif fonts in small point sizes and it is said that young people, who have been brought up reading more print in sans serif fonts than older people, do not find that sans serif text slows down their reading. However, a point to remember when considering using them is that, because of the lack of variation in line thickness, pages of sans serif fonts can look tedious. These characteristics make sans serif fonts a frequent choice for brochures or reference books that are not likely to be read from cover to cover. Compare the examples on this page.

When you become familiar with the categories you will observe that some fonts take on a different appearance when their size changes. When this occurs, some are pleasant on the eye in small sizes and others are better when large. For example, one of the well-known British banks uses, as part of its corporate image, an extremely distinctive font in its advertising and literature. It works well in headlines but is tiresome in the text of leaflets.

Package holidays have a price advantage over independent travel, comparing the cost of getting there and staying in the same hotel, because holiday operators are able to negotiate large discounts from airlines and hotel proprietors. Holiday makers who can be flexible about where and when they go stand a good chance of getting a holiday for even less.

(Times Roman)

Package holidays have a price advantage over independent travel, comparing the cost of getting there and staying in the same hotel, because holiday operators are able to negotiate large discounts from airlines and hotel proprietors. Holiday makers who can be flexible about where and when they go stand a good chance of getting a holiday for even less.

(Elementary)

Font categories

Old Style fonts

Old style fonts developed from handwriting using quills or wedge-tipped pens. They therefore have serifs, which are the little tails at the extremities of letters such as these from the Charter font I am using for my normal (body) text, or from Times Roman, which is perhaps more familiar, or Bookman Old Style, which isn't.

Modern Serif fonts

These have serifs that are more horizontal or slab-like. 'Modern' is a relative term: they started to be developed in the nineteenth century. Examples are: Courier, **Albertus** and **Palermo**.

Sans Serif fonts

In the early twentieth century, fonts with an uncluttered appearance were designed. They are known by the French term *sans serif* (without serif). Examples are: Arial, Century Gothic and Elementary.

Script fonts

Script fonts mimic handwriting. For example: *Karman*, *Aristocrat* and *Lucinda Handwriting*.

Decorative and Display fonts

Decorative fonts, of which there is an enormous number, often seem to have been designed on the principle of 'the weirder the better', although some have a long pedigree in the history of printing in certain parts of the world. Some examples are: UMBRA, ALGERIAN, Frankenstein and Hobbit. There are some fonts, primarily decorative, but particularly designed for posters and headlines, called display fonts. They always work best in large sizes, and so look strange in these examples: Playbill and Americana. To see how much better these fonts look when larger, see them on page 73 and the front cover of the book respectively.

Font style and legibility

A third consideration for legibility is the style (not to be confused with *paragraph* style) of font used. This refers to whether the font is 'ordinary' (technically called 'roman' [not capitalised], but sometimes 'regular' or 'normal'), italic (sometimes called 'oblique', especially when it refers to sans serif fonts), bold (or 'black') and italic bold.

In *Quick Bits* you learned the uses of italics and bold text, but now I will explain why they look different. Proper italic and bold characters are designed to be different from the roman characters of the same font, and italics are not the same as script fonts:

- Bold characters are designed with thicker lines: sans serif fonts are heavy all over; serif fonts are heavy on the downstrokes.
- Italic versions of serif fonts often have distinctly different forms for letters such as 'a' and 'f'.
- Bold and italic characters occupy different amounts of space from the roman forms because of their shapes.

Compare the examples at the top of the opposite page.

Some old word processors slant roman characters electronically in imitation of italics but, of course, the shapes of the letters do not change.

In *Quick Bits* it was suggested that quotations of about three or more lines in length should *not* be set in italics because they become more difficult to read. The same consideration applies to script fonts. Look inside the front cover of a British passport for an example. The roman form of a font is usually the easiest to read.

Subtle messages to readers

Now let's conduct a little experiment. Cover up the four sentences opposite and uncover them one at a time. As you do so, think where you might expect to see such a sentence.

Turn the page to see my suggestions.

Font styles: roman, bold and italic

Century Schoolbook: abcdefghijklmnopqrstuvwxyz
Century Schoolbook: abcdefghijklmnopqrstuvwxyz
Century Schoolbook: abcdefghijklmnopqrstuvwxyz

Century Gothic: abcdefghijklmnopqrstuvwxyz
Century Gothic: abcdefghijklmnopqrstuvwxyz
Century Gothic: abcdefghijklmnopqrstuvwxyz

Dr Kraskov was certain that the arm could be sewn on.

Dr Kraskov was certain that the arm could be sewn on.

Dr Kraskov was certain that the arm could be sewn on.

𝔇r 𝔎raskov was certain that the arm could be sewn on.

How about, in turn:

- From an official investigation report.
- From a magazine article about modern surgery.
- From a detective novel.
- From the cover of a video cassette.

Even if you do not agree with my suggestions you will have understood the point that different fonts convey different messages.

Old style serif fonts convey a message of authority that is traditional and conservative.

Sans serif fonts carry a different kind of authority, one that is modern, technical and scientific.

Modern serif fonts vary tremendously. Some are similar to old style serif fonts and some are close to decorative ones. While modern serif fonts that are similar to old style can appear at first sight to be an attractive change for text, their unfamiliarity may have an unsettling effect on readers.

Script and decorative fonts tend to be used for special effects, particularly in advertising. In *all* contexts they should be used with great restraint: if the reader notices the font rather than the message in the words, your communication has been blocked. More word processors will soon allow decorative effects to be applied to 'ordinary' fonts. Effects such as rotating words, giving them shadows, printing white on black or squeezing them into fancy shapes. Use these with even more caution than decorative fonts.

Technological developments have long affected the fashionable usage of particular fonts. Have you noticed, for example, that it is possible to tell the decade in which a film was made by the style of the titles? With each change of technology in the titling studios, new effects were enthusiastically applied until the next change came along.

What to do now

Redefine, a number of times, the normal (body text) style in your document to change the font category. You cannot properly judge the effect on the screen, so print pages each time. Compare them with the copy you printed at the end of *Quick Bits*. I am sure you now appreciate the power of styles: one change and the whole document changes. It is much easier than going through it changing one paragraph after another!

When you have finished experimenting, decide on the impression you want your document to convey and choose a serif or sans serif font for the normal text, in an appropriate point size. Before you throw away your next junk mail, consider the fonts that the advertisers have chosen to use and why. Better still, collect examples of leaflets where you think fonts have been well or poorly chosen.

Decorative and script fonts: Ramona, Playbill and Aristocrat

Come to Mr Kite's Ball!

Wanted! Dead or Alive!

Wedding Invitation

Decorative effects applied to Charter font

flying

2.8. Mixing fonts

Mixing fonts in a document can be tricky, but make a refined touch if done well.

In general, when mixing fonts, choose ones that are very distinct. The more similar they are, the more they are likely to clash. Conversely, the more dissimilar the fonts, the better they tend to work together. Therefore, choose fonts from different categories and increase the difference between them with differences in size or font style (roman, bold or italic). See the table opposite.

Be restrained in the use of more than one font in a document. Where mixing *can* be useful is to distinguish between the body text and headings, tables, headers, footers, and text on the covers of documents, as we will explore in later sections.

In leaflets and advertisements there is more scope for mixing fonts and using decorative fonts for effect. Even then it is good to practise restraint. There are some further comments and examples in *Part 6, Worked Examples*.

If in doubt about how well two fonts complement each other, stick to one.

2.9. The look of headings

Do you remember from the *Quick Bits* section that the relative importance of headings to each other should be indicated by variations of three elements: the point size, the weight of the text and the font used and that at that time we only dealt with the first two? Now you know about legibility and the messages that font types convey, we can think about the use of different fonts in headings.

Having a different font for a heading gently livens up documents that would otherwise be rather boring in appearance. It works best if you use a serif font for the bulk of text (to make it easy for people to read) and a sans serif one for headings, to convey an impression of clarity. It can be the other way round if your main text needs a sans serif font. What do you think of the look of the headings that I chose for this book?

Opposite are three examples of headings and text.

What to do now

Earlier in this book you went through your experimental document and applied styles to different levels of headings. Now use the style facility to experiment with different fonts in headings.

Because styles enable changes to be made to the look of each instance of a heading in one go, they help ensure consistency throughout the document — and you remember how important that is! You can keep changing your mind about a look until you find one you like.

Increasingly different fonts

This text is set in
10 point Times Roman

This text is set in
10 point Footlight Light

This text is set in
10 point Book Antiqua
Italic

```
This text is set
in 10 point
Courier
```

This text is set in
10 point Palermo

This text is set in
10 point Technical Italic

This text is set in
10 point Elementary

This text is set in
10 point Arial

This text is set in
10 point Lucinda
Sans Italic

This text is set in 10 point
Monotype Corsiva

This text is set in
10 point Aristocrat

This text is set in
10 point Lucinda
Handwriting

This text is set in 10 point
Cloister Black

This text is set in
10 point Ramona

This text is set in
10 point Poster
Bodoni

Heading and body text contrasts

This heading is set in Bookman Old Style

It clashes with this text, which is set in Book Antigua as both are old style serif fonts. The letters of this typeface are more compact and less rounded than those of the heading. Compare the word 'Book' and the shapes of the letters 'e' and 'a'. Both fonts clash with the Charter font that is used for the main text on the page.

This heading is set in Montreal Bold

This text is still set in Book Antigua but because the character of the font used for the heading is very different, it works. The Montreal is sans serif and, being set in bold, it happens to give the impression of being approximately the same compactness as this text.

This heading is set in Montreal

This example is the same as the one above, except, just to see the effect, I have used the roman font for the heading, rather than the bold one. It still works, but as the heading is not quite so solid it does not compete as strongly with the text. It therefore looks weaker and does not hold your attention so well. This shows the value of experimenting.

2.10. Tables

To set up a table comprising rows and columns on a manual typewriter it was necessary to use the tab key to move the paper carriage to the same spot each time. Spaces had to be inserted in front of numbers to line them up if the number of digits they contained varied. Some people still apply this principle to their word processing. Although using spaces to align items worked on a typewriter without proportional letter spacing, it is doomed to failure on a word processor because, usually, the digits are different widths.

Instead of using tabs, word processors can insert tables, each cell of which can be manipulated differently. Unfortunately, very few people seem to use that facility to its full advantage.

The example opposite develops in stages to illustrate the process. It starts with the text and numbers in the most basic table form. The gridlines between the cells, such as you might see on the screen but which do not print, have been shown as broken lines, for clarity.

Stage 1
The plain text has been put into the table.

Stage 2
The font has been changed to a sans serif one.

The changed font gives the table a 'clean' look, differentiating it from the general text and making later alignment of the numbers easier. To improve alignment, check whether the font you wish to use has digits of equal width. To do this, type a line of ten or so 1's and, directly underneath, the same number of 0's. If they do not finish at the same point, choose another font whose numbers do.

Because the apparent size of sans serif fonts is generally larger than serif ones, the point size has been reduced from 12 to 10.5 (the precise reduction is not crucial). The font change is made at an early stage because it will affect later formatting. The font and size can be set up as a style ('table body', for example) for consistency throughout the document.

Stage 3
The middle rows of the table have been automatically sorted in alphabetical order on the first column, and en dashes used to replace the hyphens in the 'Notes' column.

The text in the header row has been centred. The pound signs are separated from the rest of the text by inserting soft breaks (see page 62).

Stage 1

Item	Price per item £	Quantity	Total Cost £	Notes
Pen	11.50	6	69.00	Green only
Eraser	0.30	30	9.00	-
Sharpener	0.62	10	6.20	Out of stock
Pencil	0.10	120	12.00	-
Stapler	7.80	1	7.80	-
Total			104.00	

Stage 2

Item	Price per item £	Quantity	Total Cost £	Notes
Pen	11.50	6	69.00	Green only
Eraser	0.30	30	9.00	-
Sharpener	0.62	10	6.20	Out of stock
Pencil	0.10	120	12.00	-
Stapler	7.80	1	7.80	-
Total			104.00	

Stage 3

Item	Price per item £	Quantity	Total Cost £	Notes
Eraser	0.30	30	9.00	–
Pen	11.50	6	69.00	Green only
Pencil	0.10	120	12.00	–
Sharpener	0.62	10	6.20	Out of stock
Stapler	7.80	1	7.80	–
Total			104.00	

Stage 4

The numbers in the cells below the header in columns two, three and four have been aligned within their cells by using decimal tabs.

Note that numbers in tables look best if they are aligned so that the longest numbers in the columns (in this case, 11.50, 120 and 104.00) are positioned centrally, leaving the shorter numbers with more space to their left than their right.

Stage 5

Cell borders have been switched on to start to create a 'look' for the table. For clarity, I have stopped printing the gridlines.

Stage 6

Having decided that I want stronger-looking tables, I shaded the header row and make the outer border a double line. I also make the header text bold so that it will compete with the shading. The table is completed with an automatically numbered caption in the same font as the table body text.

You have to be cautious with shading. What may be reasonable from a printer may not photocopy well on the office copier.

In the way demonstrated above, the look that you want for your tables can be built up so that they hold their own as a visual feature of your document. Some word processors have a built-in table formatting function that gives a selection of layouts that you can apply to your tables. If you have it, this will be worth experimenting with. You may find a style you like. The important thing, as with everything in this book, is to understand what effect your choice may have on the reader.

For example, in Microsoft Word 6, there are 34 pre-formatted table styles. They vary from the very simple to 3D embossed effects such as the one I have applied below to the example table. Note, however, that the automatic formatting does not make any of the design decisions that I made before the fifth stage above. It would be possible, therefore, for someone (not you!) to use this feature and still end up with messy-looking tables.

Automatically formatted table

Item	Price per item £	Quantity	Total Cost £	Notes
Eraser	0.30	30	9.00	–
Pen	11.50	6	69.00	Green only
Pencil	0.10	120	12.00	–
Sharpener	0.62	10	6.20	Out of stock
Stapler	7.80	1	7.80	–
Total			104.00	

Stage 4.

Item	Price per item £	Quantity	Total Cost £	Notes
Eraser	0.30	30	9.00	–
Pen	11.50	6	69.00	Green only
Pencil	0.10	120	12.00	–
Sharpener	0.62	10	6.20	Out of stock
Stapler	7.80	1	7.80	–
Total			104.00	

Stage 5.

Item	Price per item £	Quantity	Total Cost £	Notes
Eraser	0.30	30	9.00	–
Pen	11.50	6	69.00	Green only
Pencil	0.10	120	12.00	–
Sharpener	0.62	10	6.20	Out of stock
Stapler	7.80	1	7.80	–
Total			104.00	

Stage 6.

Table 1. Order summary

Item	Price per item £	Quantity	Total Cost £	Notes
Eraser	0.30	30	9.00	–
Pen	11.50	6	69.00	Green only
Pencil	0.10	120	12.00	–
Sharpener	0.62	10	6.20	Out of stock
Stapler	7.80	1	7.80	–
Total			104.00	

Other uses for tables

Tables are extremely useful for anchoring text on a page when you want to list something in two or more columns. Often it is much easier than using the column command. The in-cell formatting capabilities also make it more flexible than columns.

Opposite are two examples. The first illustrates a list of people's names in two columns to save space at the top of notes of a meeting or on a distribution list. This may not seem easier than tabbing across at first, but it makes it much easier to re-arrange the names if necessary after typing them in.

Some word processors will not sort text in lists into alphabetical order, but will do so if the text is contained in table cells.

The second example is from a document on which a colleague and I collaborated in preparing for print. The bulk of the given text, covering eighteen pages, was short pieces of commentary usually followed by several, longer quotations which were set in italics. The effect was difficult to read and therefore off-putting. After some experimentation we solved the problem by doing three things:

1. We left the commentary text in a serif font justified to both margins and we put it into the left-hand cells of a three-column table.
2. We re-set the quotation text in a sans serif font (that also had a lighter density than the commentary text) and left-justified it. The quotations were therefore visually distinct without clashing.
3. We put the quotations in the right-hand cells of the table, leaving the middle column to form a gutter between the text, the left edge of which was reinforced by the right hand edge of the commentary text.

Each set of quotations therefore always lined up with the relevant commentary. This would have been very difficult to achieve using columns. In the finished document this arrangement made it possible for readers to scan either the commentary or the quotations, or to take their time and read the commentary and quotations together.

What to do now

Re-format the first table in your document using the principles you learned in this section. When you have worked out a style you like, apply it to any other tables. Be consistent!

If you have used tabs to create a column of text, use a table instead.

Table used for text: Agenda distribution list (gridlines printed)

Ivor Windsor (Chair)	Chester Field
T Able	Ann T Macassar
Win Doe	Ash Trey

Table used for text: Report

An increase in responsibility and independence was viewed positively by those considering rehousing needs.	'I could manage on my own if someone would just give me a bit of support.'
The area where people live is also important.	'My worry is about people being stuck on their own in tower blocks. It takes me all of my time to get myself out and I feel like I'm running the gauntlet from my front door to the bus stop. For people who don't look ordinary, its terrible. The kids set on them and they don't want to come out at all.'

2.11. Checklist

Once again, use the checklist opposite and re-run a spell check.

Having finished the section you are ready to reprint your document so that you can compare it with the old.

Checklist of the points covered in this section

Subject	Page
Setting up and manipulating named styles for paragraphs, lists, headings, etc.	44
The advantages of numbering headings and paragraphs automatically.	46
The benefits of automatically numbering other features of your document and of inserting automatic contents and indexes.	48
Identifying three different types of lists and the do's and don'ts of presenting them.	52
Why your choice of justification affects the reader.	54
How to hyphenate your text, and why.	56
Managing 'widows and orphans'.	60
Managing 'hangers-on and danglers'.	62
How font categories, sizes and styles affect legibility.	66
The subtle messages your choice of fonts sends to readers.	70
When and when not to mix fonts in a document.	74
Improving the look of headings by changing fonts.	74
Controlling the look of tables, and some other uses for them.	76

Part 3. Managing Space

In the *Quick Bits* section you learned about the little details which, if you neglect them, will let down the smart image you are trying to put across in your documents.

In *Managing Text*, we explored some powerful ways of getting and keeping control of a document through paragraph styles, the importance of dealing with how lines end, and the effects that your choice of fonts have.

In this section, we concentrate on the aspect of managing space that is intimately associated with lines of text: that is, the kind of space that moves if the text is moved. For most people, space in a document 'just happens'. It occurs when the margins are set and when there are gaps between paragraphs. To people who produce impressive documents, space is something to control and plan.

Text has two dimensions, horizontal and vertical, and space can vary in both. As it changes, it has an impact on the legibility of the text. You will recall from the previous section how important legibility is to the unwritten, as well as the written, messages that you send to readers.

The horizontal dimension has fewer variables than the vertical, so the following two sections deal with that first.

3.1. Letterspacing (tracking)

When a font designer decides on the shape of a character, he or she leaves some space either side of it. This is called 'letterspacing' or 'tracking'. Without it all letters would touch each other, making recognition difficult. With electronic text manipulation, as well as in traditional typesetting, it is possible to vary that space.

When letterspacing is reduced, the text is compressed horizontally: printers call this 'tight'. When it is expanded, so is the whole text. Printers call this 'loose'. Note that these processes do not affect the point size of the text and that compressing in this way should not be confused with using 'condensed fonts' where the shapes of the characters have been re-designed to be narrower than normal.

This text has reduced letterspacing. It is very tight.

This text has normal letterspacing. It is neither tight nor loose.

This text has expanded letterspacing. It is very loose.

When word processors justify text to both margins they automatically manipulate space between words. How evenly the software does this will determine how smooth or how 'holey' the spaces in the lines appear.

To people who produce impressive documents, space is something to control and plan.

When might you want to deliberately change the font designer's carefully chosen letterspacing? Sometimes the only possible way of fitting a piece of text into a particular layout is to tighten or loosen the letterspacing. *If* the change is minimal, *and if* a large block of text is manipulated, it is possible to adjust the letterspacing without readers noticing. It should only be done as a last resort.

Tightening or loosening is most often used to achieve effects in blocks of text in logos, advertisements and labels. These uses are illustrated in the worked examples at the end of the book.

3.2. Kerning

Whereas 'tightening and loosening' is the technical term for wholesale adjustment of letterspacing, 'kerning' refers to adjusting the space between particular *pairs* of characters only.

The reason for doing this is that the space the font designer puts around characters produces an uncomfortable visual gap in some letter combinations. When, for example, there are two straight or sloping lines, or two rounded shapes together. These spaces usually matter only when large point sizes are in use and so kerning is usually only done for headlines, large text in advertisements or document covers.

In the example on the opposite page, the upper word is unkerned and the spaces between the letters 'Ava' and 'abl' appear to be larger than the other spaces in the word, giving it an uneven appearance. In the word beneath, those spaces have been slightly reduced to make them more even. If you are unsure of the difference, look at how the serifs in 'Ava' now overlap each other. I also thought about reducing the space between the letters 'le', although I did not do it. What do you think?

Letters are best kerned manually to obtain the desired space adjustment. The way to do it is to select the first of the letters involved and, using the word processor's 'character spacing' (or equivalent) command, change the letterspacing.

Some word processors can be instructed to automatically kern letter pairs when they occur. They have a 'table' of commonly kerned character pairs which (unknown to the user) is consulted to see whether kerning should be applied. As you might expect, word processing software varies tremendously on whether, and how well, they do this. It is enough to know that manual kerning should be considered when setting a word or piece of text in a large size — over 24 points, say.

Available

Available

What to do now

Check with your word processor manual or on-screen help whether your software allows you to change the letterspacing or to automatically kern letters. If it does, experiment a little to see the effect that each has on the text of your document, but, unless your experimentation makes an improvement (in which case build it into the paragraph style you are using), return to normal letterspacing when you have finished.

3.3. Leading (rhymes with heading)

We are now starting to deal with the vertical dimension of space connected to text.

Do you remember that fonts are measured in point sizes from the ascender line to the descender line? As there are 72 points to an inch, a 12 point font is one-sixth of an inch tall. However, if there were no extra space between lines of text the descenders and ascenders could touch each other, as in the top example opposite.

In normal 'single spaced' text, about twenty per cent extra points' worth of space is put between the lines to separate them. Normally, therefore, in text using a 12 point font, the distance between the top of the ascenders on one line to the top of the ascenders on the next would be about 14.5 points. This is illustrated in the middle example. If, instead, the font used were 20 point, the distance between the tops of ascenders would be 24 points. On a word processor the space is added electronically, but in the days of metal type, strips of lead were used. The space between lines is still, therefore, referred to as 'leading' — hence the title of this section.

The first of the examples is defined as '12 point on 12 point' (12/12); the second, 12/14.5. Some word processors just give a choice of 'single', 'one and a half' or 'double' spacing. If, however, your word processor allows you more direct control of leading, you can achieve more precise effects: the bottom example is set at 12/17.

You are probably asking *why* you should want to control the leading in this way. The answer is that, depending on the size and appearance of the font, changing the leading can improve the legibility of the text.

Zero leading

Guide dogs for people who are
registered blind are not
infrequent on our streets, but
would you know if you had
seen a hearing dog for the deaf?
Yes... they do exist!

'Single' spacing

Guide dogs for people who are
registered blind are not
infrequent on our streets, but
would you know if you had
seen a hearing dog for the deaf?
Yes... they do exist!

Set at 12/17

Guide dogs for people who are
registered blind are not
infrequent on our streets, but
would you know if you had
seen a hearing dog for the deaf?
Yes... they do exist!

In the first four blocks of the example opposite, the font size is 8 point. The first of those blocks is set at 8/9.5 (that is, normal spacing); the second at 8/12; the third at 8/14. These examples illustrate that as space between lines becomes larger, the eye can take in small letters more easily. There comes a time however, that with excessively large space, as in the fourth block at 8/30, the eye has to search for the next line, disrupting the flow and decreasing legibility.

Within limits, therefore, text in small font sizes, particularly sans serif fonts, becomes more legible with extra space.[*] The opposite effect can happen with text in very large point sizes, such as might be used in headlines: decreasing the space between lines from normal can *improve* legibility. The fifth block of the example is set at 50/60 (that is, single, or twenty per cent leading) and the final block is set at 50/52 (four per cent).

What to do now

Find out how much control your software allows you to have over leading.

Look through the last printed version of your document making a quick visual check of any places where it might be appropriate to subtly change the space between the lines and do so if you can, leaving the body text in single spacing. Otherwise, as before, experiment a little to see the effect of changing the leading of your body text, and leave it as you like best.

[*] In advertisements in particular, you will notice that the relative size of the font and leading will be pushed to extremes for particular design effects and, perhaps, to slow readers down and hold their attention for longer.

Legibility varies with leading

Guide dogs for people who are registered
blind are not infrequent on our streets, but
would you know if you had seen a hearing
dog for the deaf? Yes... they do exist!

Guide dogs for people who are registered
blind are not infrequent on our streets, but
would you know if you had seen a hearing
dog for the deaf? Yes... they do exist!

Guide dogs for people who are registered
blind are not infrequent on our streets, but
would you know if you had seen a hearing
dog for the deaf? Yes... they do exist!

Guide dogs for people who are registered

blind are not infrequent on our streets, but

would you know if you had seen a hearing

dog for the deaf? Yes... they do exist!

Apple pie, or pie in the sky?

Apple pie, or pie in the sky?

3.4. Inter-paragraph spacing

As well as considering space between lines, we must consider space above, below and between blocks of text.

Most people using a word processor have the line spacing set to single. To end paragraphs they press the Enter key (↵) twice: once to finish the line, and once to create a blank one. If you add up how many points of *apparent* space this creates, the gap appears much more than the 'single line' that people suppose they are inserting. For example, if the point size is 12, the apparent gap can be 20 – 24 points between the 'x' height baseline of the top paragraph and the top of the 'x' height of the following one.

It is well established that paragraphs separated by space look better if the gaps are approximately equal to, or slightly less than, the gap that would have been left if there were just an invisible row of text. That means that *most documents* being produced these days would look better if the space between paragraphs were reduced. How?

If your word processor only allows fixed spacing, then the answer is to reduce the point size of the 'blank line' between paragraphs. Instead of a 12 point line, try one which is 4, 5 or 6 points high. However, going through a document changing the point size of all those blank lines is a tremendous task. Even assigning a 'named style' containing the reduced point size is still a huge task the first time through: it just makes it easier later to change everything to another size if you decide to alter it.

Controlling the inter-paragraph space is very easy, however, if your word processor allows you to add space before and after a paragraph. You simply re-define the paragraph style so that the required (say, five or six) points of space are added above it. Now when Enter is pressed at the end of a paragraph, the extra space you have defined is automatically added. The paragraphs are separated by this space so you do not need to press Enter again — you are ready to begin typing the next paragraph! In this example opposite, to illustrate the difference, the end of paragraph marker (¶) has been printed to indicate where Enter was pressed.

If you are re-working a document typed by someone else, it will be necessary to go through the document deleting the blank inter-paragraph lines they have inserted. This is not as time-consuming as it sounds and it is easier after you have added the inter-paragraph space to the normal text through re-defining the style, as the gaps will be more obvious. If your word processor has an option to display space, tab and paragraph markers on your screen, doing so will help you immediately spot the blank lines you are aiming to delete.

Reduced inter-paragraph space

Block of 12 point, single-spaced text with no space added above the paragraph. Block of 12 point, single-spaced text with no space added above the paragraph. Block of 12 point, single-spaced text with no space above the paragraph. Block of 12 point, single-spaced text¶

enter (↵) ⟶ ▶¶   } obtrusive extra space

Block of 12 point, single-spaced text with no space added above the paragraph. Block of 12 point, single-spaced text with no space added above the paragraph. Block of 12 point, single-spaced text with no space above the paragraph. Block of 12 point, single-spaced text¶
                                                                         } extra space eliminated
This paragraph separated from the other by five points of space added above it, incorporated into the paragraph style. This paragraph separated from the other by five points of space added above it, incorporated into the paragraph style. This paragraph separated from the other by five points of space added above it, incorporated into the paragraph style.¶

Other ways of marking the beginning of paragraphs

As mentioned above, the purpose of breaks between paragraphs is simply to indicate where each begins. There are other ways of doing this without putting in space. These can be useful when you want to catch the reader's eye, or when space is limited.

The least often used method is to begin each paragraph with a symbol that is indented into the left margin. This is mostly used for eye-catching purposes, on leaflets or other short pieces of text. See the top example.

The paragraphs do not form a list, and unlike a bulleted list, the horizontal space between the marker and the beginning of the text is minimal, in this case, one space wide. Suitable markers can be found in some of the more fancy character sets that you now know how to access. A variant is to line up the marker with the left hand margin and not have it stick out.

An example of this technique can be found (at the time of publication) on the reverse of National Lottery playslips. Confusingly, the paragraph marker chosen is the same dot used in one of the paragraphs as the point for a bulleted list!

The second technique, illustrated in the second example, is widely used in newspapers, magazines, newsletters and anywhere that text is arranged in narrow columns. The technique is to indent the first line of paragraphs.

Points to note about this technique are:
- The first paragraph after a heading is not indented as it is obviously the start of a paragraph.
- The indentation is only as long as an em dash: not five spaces, as taught in typing.
- Do not mix this technique with the one of leaving extra inter-paragraph space.

Do not 'tab' to achieve the first line indentation. *All* forms of indentation, positive and negative, are better built into the paragraph style. Most word processors can produce indentation where first lines of paragraphs are different from the rest.

What to do now

Include inter-paragraph space above your normal paragraphs, adding it to your normal paragraph style unless your document is formatted with narrow columns, in which case use the first-line-indented technique.

Now work through your document removing blank lines between paragraphs. It will take you some time, but *do not skip this task*. While you are at it, remove any blank lines you come across in lists or below headings.

Copy some of your text to a new document and try experimenting with a fancy paragraph marker.

Fancy paragraph marker

⌘ The pilot is believed to have filed a false flight plan and, after taking off from Marbella, flown an unknown route to a small airstrip. The passenger and drugs were then taken on board.
⌘ It is presumed that the crash happened as they flew low to avoid detection by radar.
⌘ A shepherd found the bodies in the wreckage of the crash when he went to look for his goats that were roaming the mountains. A hundred kilos of Moroccan hashish were lying where they had tumbled from the wrecked plane.
⌘ It was three months from the time of the crash to the time that the shepherd came across them. Some parts of Spain are still wild and uninhabited at the close of the twentieth century.

Indents marking paragraphs

The pilot is believed to have filed a false flight plan and, after taking off from Marbella, flown an unknown route to a small airstrip. The passenger and drugs were then taken on board.

It is presumed that the crash happened as they flew low to avoid detection by radar.

A shepherd found the bodies in the wreckage of the crash when he went to look for his goats that were roaming the mountains. A hundred kilos of Moroccan hashish were lying where they had tumbled from the wrecked plane.

It was three months from the time of the crash to the time that the shepherd came across them. Some parts of Spain are still wild and uninhabited at the close of the twentieth century.

3.5. Lists revisited

Now that you know about inter-paragraph spacing, you are going to improve further the look of your numbered and bulleted lists.

At the moment, in your experimental document, the paragraph that goes immediately before a list and introduces it (list header paragraph) and the list items appear as separate paragraphs. They have the same inter-paragraph spacing as your normal text. That is not quite logical, is it? They really belong together. The header paragraph and list items should, therefore, have no added space between them.

You can find examples of this variation of paragraph space in lists throughout this book.

What to do now

Select a list item, remove the added above-paragraph space and re-name the style to 'list' or 'bullet'. Work through the document selecting all list items and assigning them to the new style. Everything associated with the list will now be grouped together.

When next typing up a new document this process will be easier because you can define the style at the beginning and assign the list items it to as you go along.

You can, if it suits your font or the overall layout, add a little inter-paragraph spacing, say 2 – 3 points, back into the list items, but always keep the space distinctly less than between normal paragraphs.

3.6. Tables revisited

The final table developed as an example in Section 2.10 is reproduced opposite.

It was fine as far as it went, but now it can be improved too. The text and figures are close to the top and bottom cell borders. By adding a few points of space above and below the text and numbers we can stop it looking so cramped. Two or three points are sufficient — in the example I have used three.

What to do now

Modify the vertical space in your tables if your word processor allows it. Redefine the style to include the changed space.

Stage 6 (As previous)

Table 1. Order summary

Item	Price per item £	Quantity	Total Cost £	Notes
Eraser	0.30	30	9.00	–
Pen	11.50	6	69.00	Green only
Pencil	0.10	120	12.00	–
Sharpener	0.62	10	6.20	Out of stock
Stapler	7.80	1	7.80	–
Total			104.00	

Stage 7

Table 1. Order summary

Item	Price per item £	Quantity	Total Cost £	Notes
Eraser	0.30	30	9.00	–
Pen	11.50	6	69.00	Green only
Pencil	0.10	120	12.00	–
Sharpener	0.62	10	6.20	Out of stock
Stapler	7.80	1	7.80	–
Total			104.00	

3.7. Headings revisited

In general, a heading looks best when there is slightly more space between it and the text *above*, than there is between it and the *following* text. This arrangement sends the subtle message that the heading belongs to the following text and is not just hovering between the two. Different space should be built into the styles of each level of heading.

The nearer the heading is to the top of the hierarchy, the more space is left above it, particularly if it is also in a larger point size. If one level of heading always occurs at the top of a page (which might happen at the start of a new section or chapter) either put no additional space above, or, as is more common in the United States, a distinctively large space, say 3 – 5cm.

The varied use of space in the example opposite helps it look integrated. This table shows how the space was managed to achieve this effect. Measurements are in points. All text has single line-spacing (automatic leading) for its point size.

Style	Text font size	Extra space above
heading 1	18	page break + 0
heading 2	16	8
heading 3	14	6
heading 4	10.5	4
body	10.5	3

This combination of point sizes works for the font used in the example. With other fonts you will need to experiment with what looks best to you.

What to do now

Look at the headings in your experimental document and redefine the styles with appropriate amounts of space above and below if your word processor allows you to do it. If your word processor does not, consider inserting lines in very small point sizes between your headings and the text above them to give a small amount of separation. *This is very much a second-best option.*

Note the message in the example about indentation of the left margin to accommodate heading or paragraph numbering.

1. Heading Level 1

1.1. Heading Level 2

Some documents number headings and sub-headings. Others number the paragraphs instead, depending on the purpose or look.

The numbers will usually project into the left margin. Do not use tabs to align the blocks of text but set up the style for an indented paragraph. Allow sufficient indentation to accommodate the four numbers needed in Heading 4.

1.1.1. Heading Level 3

Some documents number headings and sub-headings. Others number the paragraphs instead, depending on the purpose or look.

1.1.1.1. Heading Level 4

Some documents number headings and sub-headings. Others number the paragraphs instead, depending on the purpose or look.

1.1.1.2. Heading Level 4

Some documents number headings and sub-headings. Others number the paragraphs instead, depending on the purpose or look.

1.2. Heading Level 2

Some documents number headings and sub-headings. Others number the paragraphs instead, depending on the purpose or look.

The numbers will usually project into the left margin. Do not use tabs to align the blocks of text but set up the style for an indented paragraph. Allow sufficient indentation to accommodate the four numbers needed in Heading 4.

1.2.1. Heading Level 3

Some documents number headings and sub-headings. Others number the paragraphs instead, depending on the purpose or look.

1.2.1.1. Heading Level 4

Some documents number headings and sub-headings. Others number the paragraphs instead, depending on the purpose or look.

1.2.1.2. Heading Level 4

Some documents number headings and sub-headings. Others number the paragraphs instead, depending on the purpose or look.

1.3. Heading Level 2

1.3.1. Heading Level 3

Some documents number headings and sub-headings. Others number the paragraphs instead, depending on the purpose or look.

3.8 Checklist

After consulting the checklist opposite and running a spell check, reprint your document.

The changes may appear less dramatic than after the previous sections, but the improved management of space is an important step towards producing an impressive document.

Subject	Page
Vary letterspacing (tracking) for effect, but not to save space, except as a last resort.	84
Kern letters that are in large point sizes.	86
To improve legibility of text: increase leading (pronounced 'ledding') for text in small point sizes, decrease it for text in large sizes.	88
Use inter-paragraph spacing that does not create a gap as wide as produced by a single blank line. Build it into your 'normal' paragraph style.	92
Instead of space between paragraphs, consider using indents or symbols to mark their beginnings, especially when using narrow columns.	94
To maintain the visual integrity of lists, manage the leading between the items.	96
In tables, put equal amounts of space above and below numbers and text.	96
Manage inter-paragraph spacing above and below headings to connect them visually to the neighbouring text.	98

Part 4. Managing the Overall Look

You have now learned nearly all that you need to make your documents look more impressive than you thought possible. The final topics are about how to choose a good layout for your document and how to achieve the total effect that you want by weaving together all the things you have learned.

4.1. Basic approaches

There are two approaches to developing the look of a document. The first is to decide on the layout of a basic page as a framework before you start. The text is then fitted into the layout. This is easier if you are the author of the document, so that you can tailor what you write to fit the layout. The second approach is to assemble the final, approved text in a form that pays little attention to layout and then to find a look that suits the text and purpose of the document. We will concentrate on this approach because, if you can manage that, the former is easy.

What to do now

We will now pretend that your experimental document is one you have been given for production of the final version. Go through the checklists at the end of the earlier sections to ensure that all the details in the document have been sorted out and give it a final spell check. Save the document and save it again with a new name. Work on one version and keep the other as a safety net.

You may want to turn your computer off while you read through this section of the book.

4.2. Factors to consider

When developing a look for a document consider:
- The purpose of the document and the image you want to create.
- The likely age of the readers.
- Production constraints.
- Pictures, diagrams or tables to be inserted whose size will be difficult for you to vary.

Purpose and image

The layout of the document will be influenced by a combination of the purpose and the image that you want it to put across. Opposite, and carried on to page 105, are some examples. Note how documents that have an apparently similar purpose might need to be treated differently.

Purpose and image related to the look of documents

Purpose	Desired image	Effect on look
Company annual report.[*]	Public image of a young, lively, dynamic company.	Lots of graphics; generous use of space; clashing colours; sans serif fonts; text broken up into boxes.
Company annual report.	Public image of a safe, conservative company.	Restrained use of graphics; Old Style serif fonts; sober colours; book-like presentation.
Internal report analysing situations or suggesting strategies.	Author needs to appear authoritative as he or she wishes to influence colleagues or superiors.	Serif fonts; frequent and clear headings; line and font size chosen to aid rapid reading by busy people.
Report, as above, but to influence other companies or interested parties. If the document is for limited distribution the company will either only produce photo-copied versions or ask a printer to produce copies from laser-printed, word processed text. This is when people who create *impressive documents* will excel!	Company needs to appear authoritative and business-like.	Similar considerations to previous document, but if the report is predominantly technical, the use of a sans serif font for the body text may be considered.

(Table continued on page 105)

[*] For something as important as an annual report, most companies use a graphic designer (perhaps via a printer) to do the layout and typography. Such a designer will have access to a wide selection of graphics and have the technology and experience to produce a slick job. However, after having read this book you will be able to do two important things. One, give the designer a good text to work with by having made sure that all the details dealt with in *Quick* Bits are correct and two, you will have a better eye for what the designer has done with the text and be better able to judge the quality of the design.

Age of readers

The age of the people who are expected to read the document should have an impact on your thinking:

- Children: Lots of interesting graphics; varied decorative fonts; large point sizes (15+ depending on age).
- Teenagers: Small point sizes (7 – 10); sans serif fonts are as acceptable as serif ones; adventurously placed boxes of text; narrow margins. Young people are used to quite sophisticated graphics, so it would be easy to patronise them by attempts to make things look fashionable or lively. If in doubt, keep it simple.
- Adults: Middle point sizes (10 – 13); emphasis on legibility, clarity and ease-of-reading.
- Older people: Moderately large point sizes (13 – 14).

Production constraints

You will need to consider whether your document is to be single- or double-sided. If is to be double-sided, your page layout planning will have to take account of the visual effect of the opposing pages on each other, as I had to for this book.

The type of binding to be used will affect how much extra room you will need to leave down the inner page margins.

If your document is to be produced by a printing firm directly from your copy, you need to be aware that printers work on sheets of paper that can be folded two, four or eight times. The whole document, including any introductory pages but not counting the covers if they are to be printed separately, is therefore easier to print and bind (and therefore less expensive) if it is designed to fit a number of pages that is divisible by four, eight or sixteen respectively. This consideration may affect the size of your margins or of the font and leading you choose.

Pictures, diagrams and tables

Pictures, diagrams and tables are all strong visual elements that you will need to consider when you place them on a page. Sometimes it is not possible to re-size them to fit neatly into your layout. If that is the case, it is better for them to obviously not fit, which looks like a deliberate design feature, rather than to 'not quite fit', which looks like a mistake. Devices such as separating these objects from the main text by a ruled line, or letting the text wrap around, may help prevent them looking too out of place.

As with everything in this book, *be consistent*. Tables are sometimes the hardest thing to lay out in a consistent way as it may be possible to fit small ones neatly into your text, but you may have one or two that you cannot reduce in size. Either make them all big, or have two distinct table formats, one for small and one for big tables.

Table continued from page 103

Internal newsletter.	As well as *informing* staff, the aim is to build up or maintain their confidence in the company. Staff see a company's weaknesses from the inside. What-ever the messages in the text, the present-ation needs to be competent at least. In fact, 'competent' may be better than 'flashy'.	Traditional two or three column layout; bold headlines; staff photos, cartoons, etc.
Technical information leaflet.	Company wishes to appear authoritative.	Formal, centred design, possibly using columns; text justified to both margins; sans serif font; use of informative diagrams.
General information leaflet.	Company wishes to appear accessible.	Text justified to left margin only; decorative font (main heading only); humorous or informative graphics.
Overhead projector slides.	Presenter wishes to come across clearly and project an image of being competent and well organised.	Large font, serif or sans serif; reduced leading; main points only; bulleted lists. (Note: fancy backgrounds do not help give a good impression if the text is hard to read.)
Promotional letters from multinational publishing or mail order companies.	Wish to look homely, intimate and not sophisticated — that is, the opposite of what they are.	Set out as if hand-typed: courier typeface; liberal use of under-lining; capitals for emphasis; double spacing. (The companies' million-pound market research tells them this ploy works. Who are we to argue?)

4.3. Layout design

Why bother to work the text of a document into an interesting or attractive layout? Having read this far, you probably believe that this is worth doing to produce a really impressive document. It would also be legitimate to want to show off your new skills to best advantage. There is a more compelling reason, however.

Millions of documents are produced each week where text is churned out between 26mm (one inch) margins and, despite being split up by headings, they look absolutely boring. Most people on the receiving end of these documents put them aside to read later and often never do unless they are obliged to wade through them. The contents of the documents may be fascinating but there is no incentive to read. If the documents were produced in this way *on purpose*, the recipients would feel insulted. Readers only put up with it because they know as little about the capabilities of word processors as the people that produce the documents!

Laying out pages in an interesting way has several purposes:
- It attracts the reader.
- It enables and encourages the reader to keep reading.
- It tells the reader that you value the time and effort that he or she is spending reading the document.
- It tells the reader about your capability and skill.

Horizontal management of the page

Across the page, most layouts are variations on one of four themes:
1. A single column of text.
2. Two equal-width column texts.
3. Three or more equal-width column texts.
4. Two columns of unequal width, with or without text in both columns.

In the illustrations, notice the space surrounding the blocks of text: graphic designers refer to such space as 'white space'. This term indicates that they are looking at it as a positive commodity, with an impact of its own. (It is still called 'white space', by the way, even if it is a coloured background!) White space defines the shape of the text and determines the overall look of the document.

Basic column layouts and variations

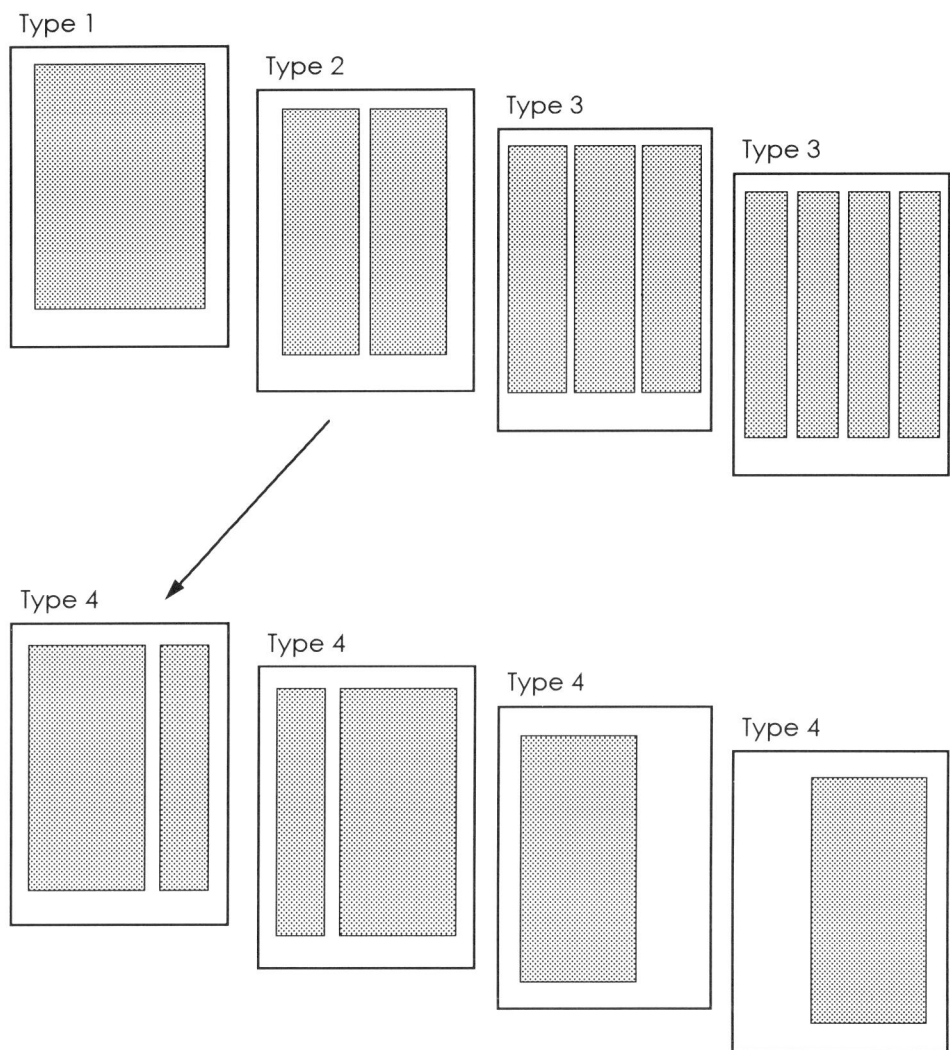

Type 1

Type 2

Type 3

Type 3

Type 4

Type 4

Type 4

Type 4

Each of the basic layouts on the previous page are described in terms of the column structure but it is just as important to think about, and *see*, the layout in terms of the white space surrounding the blocks of text, as the space 'holds' the text like a frame. Do you remember the description in *Quick Bits* of extra space between sentences as being like 'potholes'? Space tends to slow the eye down but it is essential to help the brain sort out the different parts of what it is looking at.

Managing columns

The basic layouts described above have different uses:

1. Single columns of text are what word processors produce by default. A single column of text, for reasons that will become clear later, is only really suitable for documents with small page sizes, such as books, or for short documents that may be read only once, where the recipients are likely to be highly motivated to read, such as letters.

2. Two equal-width column texts are good for formal reports and some newsletters. Double columns allow easy placement of tables and illustrations and permit the use of text in larger point sizes than do three columns.

    When working with two or more columns, legibility increases, up to a point, the wider that the gap (the gutter) is between them. Restrained use of a vertical line (rule) between the columns can also be helpful to keep readers' eyes from straying from one column to another.

    Have you noticed that, almost without exception, dictionaries use two even columns? This is not just out of convention, but it is a layout that allows short entries to occupy space efficiently.

3. Three or more equal-width column texts are commonly used as a basis for newsletters. It produces a flexible structure for pages that can be varied to double or single columns in places for variety. When using three columns, text should not be set larger than ten point. Depending on the font used, more than twenty per cent leading may be useful to improve legibility.

    Four columns with small point sizes are used to squeeze lots of text onto a page in a less-than-friendly way. To find an example you will need look no further than where firms set out their terms and conditions of trading. To be even more off-putting, they may also print the text in a light-coloured ink.

4. Two columns of unequal width, with or without text in both columns, can produce some attractive as well as useful layouts. If the narrower of the two columns contains text, it

Concentrate on doing the task in hand as well as you can. If you are working on the final layout, the time for making major changes to the text is long past.

may be contained in a box (called a sidebar) and/or differentiated from the text in the larger column by the use of a different font (as in the last example in the section on tables in 2.10). Usually it is some kind of supplementary text to the main one, such as an in-depth focus on a particular point, a quotation, or highlighted summary.

If the narrow column is left predominantly blank, it can be used to put a company logo on each page or for the placement of the occasional graphic. The visual impact of this can be intense. Otherwise, a blank column like this is known as a 'scholar's margin', the idea being that the reader has room to write notes alongside.

If the document is to be printed with pages of text facing each other, you will have to decide whether the narrow column is better on the side near, or away from, the binding.

The other design consideration is where to put headings: in the text or to the side.

Many people believe that if they reduce the width of text from a single column that goes across the whole page, to a narrower column, then the length of the document will be extended. It comes as a surprise to find that the extra is often a lot less than one expects. The reason is that the text flows into all the unused space at the ends of paragraphs and extra lines are not necessarily created. If the newly-released space on the page is used for headings, as in the upper right-hand example opposite, or for other parts of the text in boxes, space is used even more efficiently. Besides, if a slight increase in length of the document does result, the gain in legibility and the improved look will far outweigh it.

Text in columns

This important section links together factors that affect legibility, such as: the way people scan text, font style, point size, leading and hyphenation.

If you watch people as they read, you will see that their eyes do not slide smoothly along the line of text but move in a series of jerky movements as they take in batches of three to five words at a time. A long line of text therefore requires more of these movements to get to the end of the line. Within reason, the fewer movements the eye has to make to get to the end of the line, the less chance there is of readers loosing their place and the quicker the whole text can be read. Newspapers have this down to a fine art — news columns that people want to read quickly often only have three to five words on a line but other sections, such as book reviews, to be read more slowly, use wider columns with more words per line.

The ideal length of line for legibility is related to the compactness of the font used and its point size. Over the years people have worked out various formulae for calculating this length. One of

Variations on two columns of different widths

the easiest rules of thumb for achieving the ideal line length for
ease of reading is to use two and a third times the length of the
lower case alphabet in the font you are using — but it does not
have to be exact! Look at the examples opposite.

There are two ways of using this principle to present easily
legible text:

- Change the font size to fit your desired line length.
  Note: Some fonts, particularly those with an x-height that
  is tall relative to the width of the x, are not easily legible
  in point sizes below 11. You can compensate for this by
  using extra leading.
- Change the line length to suit the size of the font.

For design reasons, you may want to maintain a particular size
of font with a shorter or longer line length than rule of thumb
suggests. In either case legibility will be improved by increasing
the leading from the single spacing standard of twenty per cent
added to the font height, to thirty per cent.

When there are few words on each line, it is hard for the word
processor to avoid either making the line ends very ragged or
leaving pools of space between the words, depending on the
text justification. Therefore, the fewer words per line, the
greater the need for hyphenation to reduce wasted space.

Symmetry

The more symmetrical a layout, the more formal it looks and
vice versa. Fully justified text helps the impression of symmetry
more than left justified text.

Font, point size and line length

abcdefghijklmnopqrstuvwxyzabcdefghijklmnopqrstuvwxyzabcdefgh
The ideal line length for ease of reading is two and a third times the
length of the lower case alphabet in the font you are using.
Times New Roman 10 point.

abcdefghijklmnopqrstuvwxyzabcdefghijklmnopqrstuvwxyzabcdefgh
The ideal line length for ease of reading is two and a third times the
length of the lower case alphabet in the font you are using.
Times New Roman 12 point.

abcdefghijklmnopqrstuvwxyzabcdefghijklmnopqrstuvwxyzabcdefgh
The ideal line length for ease of reading is two and a third times the
length of the lower case alphabet in the font you are using.
Palermo 12 point.

abcdefghijklmnopqrstuvwxyzabcdefghijklmnopqrstuvwxyzabcdefgh
The ideal line length for ease of reading is two and a third times the
length of the lower case alphabet in the font you are using.
Century Gothic 12 point.

Symmetry and formality

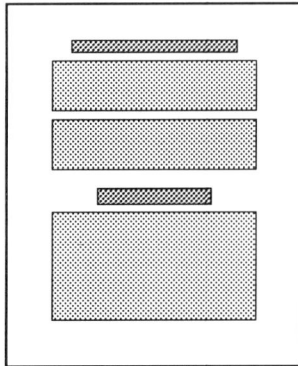

Formal

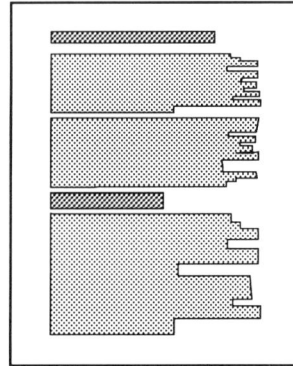

Informal

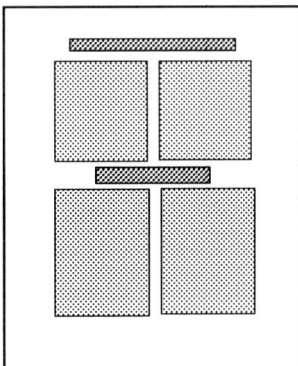

Highly formal

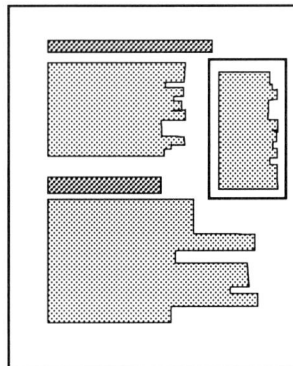

Highly informal

Vertical management of the page

So far in this section on layout, we have concentrated on what is happening across the page. What happens vertically also needs some attention.

To give documents a coherent look they need a fairly consistent page layout. In short documents, particularly leaflets and news-letters, however, the number of columns can be varied vertically on a page to make it look livelier. When this is done, the element that has the largest overall size should be on the bottom of the combination as its apparent 'weight' will give the page visual stability.

Stabilising the page

The figures on previous pages hint at the effect of headings, which break up the page vertically. To some extent the white space around the paragraphs and headings 'holds' the text on the page, but there are also other devices, particularly ruled lines (remember from Underlining in *Quick Bits*?) that can be used to add stability to layouts.

Flip through some brochures or magazines and look at the use that professional designers make of lines at the top and bottom of pages and the space that they leave around them.

If you want ruled lines to appear at the at the tops or bottoms of all pages throughout the document they are best placed in a 'header' or a 'footer'. (Look these up in your software manual if you are not familiar with them.) Doing this will make sure that they are automatically repeated in the correct position on each page.

As indicated in the bottom left-hand example opposite, headers and footers can contain information such as the page number, author's name, chapter title, date or filename. The latter two are useful in draft forms of documents.

Various combinations of columns enliven and stabilise the page

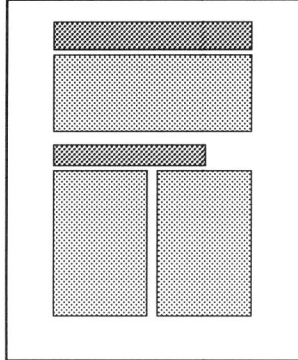

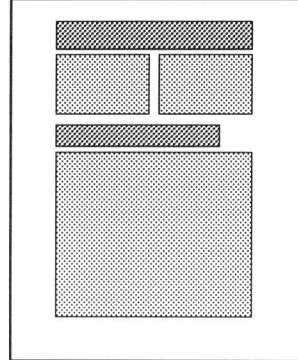

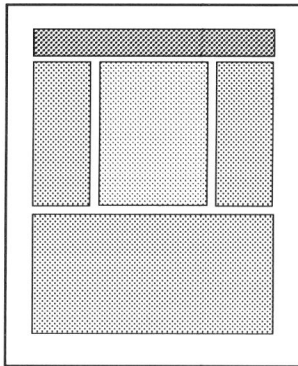

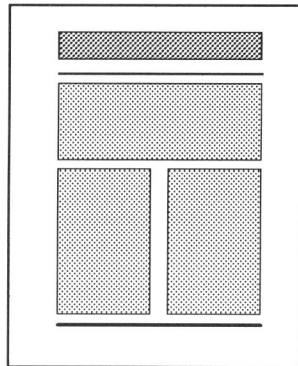

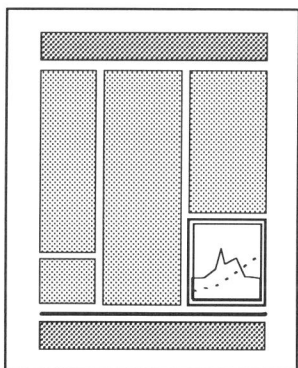

4.4. Manipulating readers' attention

There are two secret weapons that designers have in order to make document layouts look interesting. One, their knowledge of how people scan pages, and two, how that process can be controlled by adjusting the visual impact of different elements on the page.

Once you have established the basic layout of the document you can think about how to capture, and therefore direct, readers' attention to parts of the document that you think are important.

How readers scan pages

Psychological research has revealed that when readers look at a page for the first time their eyes generally glide across the top of the page from left to right, flick down to the bottom left and across to the bottom right, as in the top illustration opposite.

This pattern can be varied by 'strong visual elements' on the page (middle illustration).

If there are strong visual elements on the top of the page and in the bottom right-hand corner, readers' attention may be 'captured' and their eyes drawn back and forth across the page until they make a conscious decision to pay attention the text (bottom illustration).

An experiment

Find a magazine, sit with it in front of you and close your eyes. Open the magazine at random. Now look at the page and notice where your eyes stop first. What will have attracted them will be the element with the strongest visual impact. Your eyes will then be drawn to the element with the second strongest impact, and so on. Do this at least twenty times. Use several magazines to experience different design styles.

You will notice that professional graphic designers producing magazines and advertisements are adept at manipulating readers' attention by the use of the phenomenon of strong visual elements.

Scanning a page

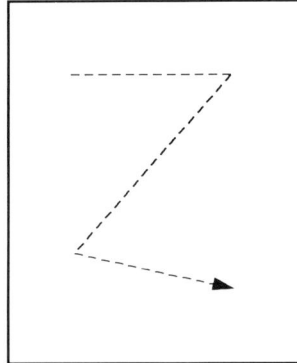

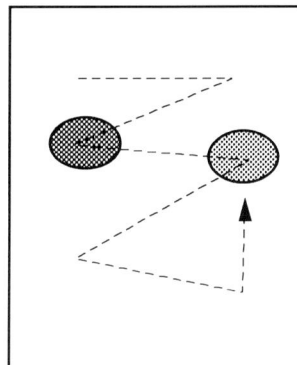

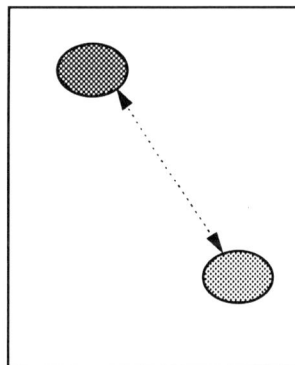

Strong visual elements

A strong visual element can be anything that attracts the eye, such as:

- A picture.
- A block of text in a box.
- A headline.
- A table or graph.
- A decorative capital at the beginning of a paragraph.
- A tiny piece of text in a large block of white space.

In general, objects that are large have a stronger visual impact than ones that are small. So do objects that are dark rather than light; objects that are coloured rather than black and white; and objects that are irregularly, rather than regularly, shaped.

Dropped and raised capitals, being big, tend to appear much stronger on a page than the rest of the text. This is even more apparent if they are set in a decorative font. They are therefore used to draw readers' eyes to the beginning of the text, inviting them to start reading.

Pictures and other graphic images make a strong visual impact. This can be intensified by placing them off-centre to the rest of the layout or by letting the text flow around them, especially if they are an irregular shape. In the latter case, allow a good margin of white space around the illustration to make it stand out. This also works for blocks of text set in a large, perhaps different, font.

Many people feel uneasy about moving tables or illustrations away from the part of the text to which they directly relate but, most readers can cope with this quite happily with the appropriate reference in the text and a caption. It may be helpful to the design to always place large tables or illustrations at the bottom of a page, perhaps separated by a rule, as a design feature.

When it is important that text does not flow from one page to another, it is necessary to insert a page break. However, this is best done as one of the last processes of laying out a document as late additions to the text or deletions from it will throw out your careful planning.

Page numbers

None of the examples so far contain page numbers. Because they are small and surrounded by space they can become strong visual elements in their own right and subtly disturb the balance of the page. This works *for* you when you want people to be able to locate pages easily, but may sometimes cause problems.

Think of ways of integrating page numbers. For example, if a rule is being used at the bottom of a page to help visual stability, you could shorten the rule slightly and locate the page number at the end, so that the rule and number form a visual unit, as illustrated opposite.

Initial capitals as strong visual elements

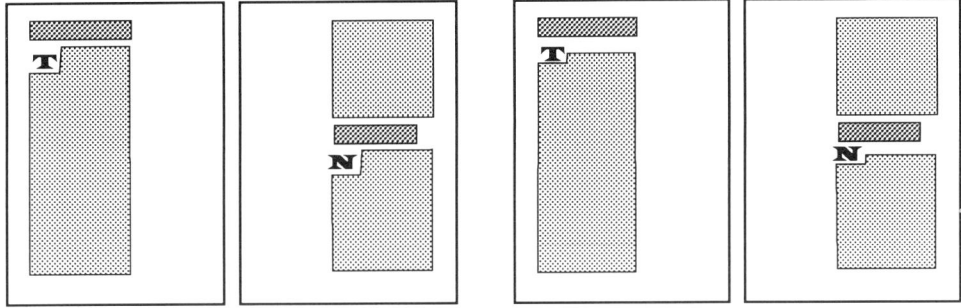

Pictures as strong visual elements

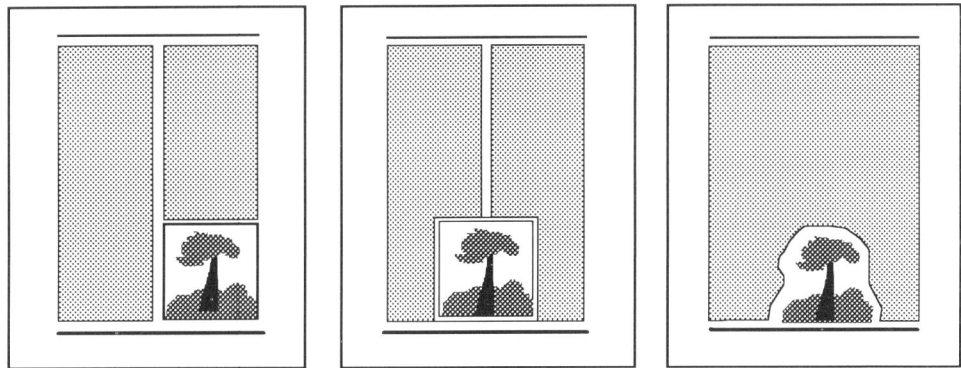

Text and tables as strong visual elements

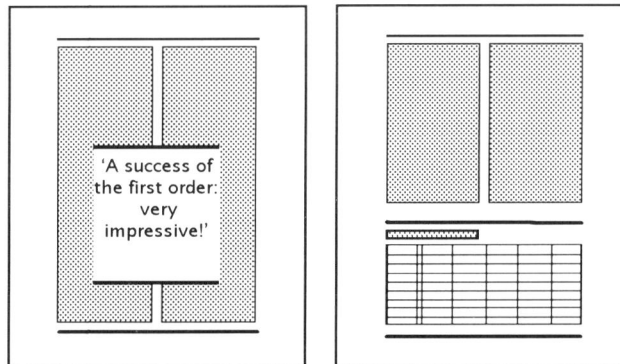

'A success of the first order: very impressive!'

Integrated page number and rule

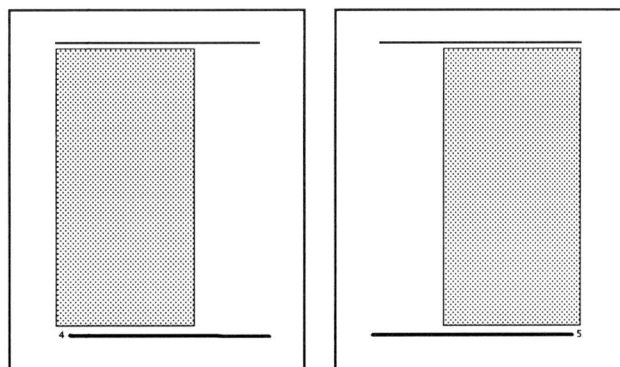

4.5. General alignment

The final point to remember about organising the elements on the page, is that it is important for the edges of the different parts to line up precisely with each other whenever possible.

Unfortunately for people setting out documents, human eyes and brains are super-sensitive when it comes to detecting slight variations. Think how your eyes are drawn to a dent in the otherwise smooth surface of a car. With text, however, large variations appear to be deliberate and therefore stop looking like mistakes.

Compare the two illustrations opposite. In the left-hand one, nothing lines up or quite fits. In the other, some discipline has been imposed, giving a much more satisfying appearance. Notice how even the headline and subhead, being left justified, now align with the edge of the text below.

Here are four tips to help to arrange a page:

- Temporarily place horizontal or vertical rules on the screen to help check the alignment of objects such as pictures.
- Most drawing software (the facility you use to insert rules) allows you to select items that you want to align and to indicate how you want them to align, that is, by making their tops, centres or sides line up. Also, the software can usually force items to fit a certain grid size ('snap to grid') when created.
- It is better to force a block of text to fill a *small* space in order to make it align with other elements on the page, than it is to leave the block unaligned. There are several strategies that can be adopted. In order of preference they are: re-write the text; change the font size; change the leading; change the letterspacing.
- Look at the printed page upside down through half-closed eyes. By shifting your attention from the subject matter of the text, you will easily spot things that do not sit comfortably on the page.

The importance of alignment

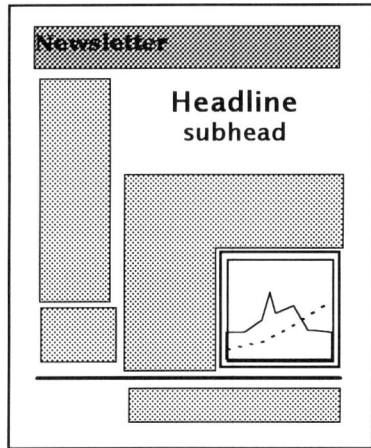

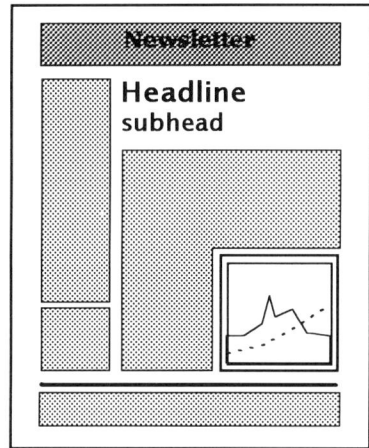

What to do now

Look at all sorts of professionally produced documents. Think about the design decisions that were made regarding the column structure of the pages and the use of constant design features such as headers and footers. Ask yourself the following questions:

- Have the column structures been varied in the documents to give stability to the layout of pages or to liven them up?
- How have illustrations been placed in relation to other strong visual elements?
- What images might the authors of the documents have wished to convey? Were the design decisions appropriate?
- How could the design be improved?
- Have the designers done things to the text or layout that this book suggests should be avoided? If so, have they done it on purpose to 'break the rules' for effect?

4.6. Checklist

Using the checklist, review the last printed version of your experimental document, asking yourself the above questions.

Make appropriate changes, run the final spell check, print a draft and check it through thoroughly. When you spot changes that you want to make, mark them with a red pen so that you will identify them easily later. In particular, pay attention to the line-ends, looking for widows and orphans, hangers-on and danglers and any places where you want to make the paragraphs less ragged (or reduce pools of space if they are fully-justified). Re-read pages 56 – 64 if you need reminding about how to deal with them.

Now make the very final changes, and print.

Compare the impressive document you have now created with the first version of the experimental document you printed at the beginning of *Quick Bits*.

Checklist of the points covered in this section

Subject	Page
Identify the purpose of the document and the image it has to project.	102
Identify the target readers, their likely ages and expectations of the document on the formal/informal dimension, etc.	104
Identify any final production constraints that may affect the layout, particularly the type of binding to be used.	104
Identify any potentially constraining design factors in the document itself — tables and diagrams, for example.	104
Make decisions about the document's basic horizontal look. That is, how many columns to use for the fundamental format and how wide they will be; whether any particular features such as a text box (sidebar) or logo will appear on each page; where to put the page numbers.	106
Take control of the vertical dimension of each page in turn, thinking about where you want readers' attention directed and checking the effect that facing pages have on each other.	114
Check the alignment of items on each page.	120

Part 5. The Whole Process

This section summarises all the things you have learned. Use it to help you apply that learning to all your forthcoming documents.

Here is the complete process:

1. Ensure that all the points in *Quick Bits* have been incorporated and that the document is consistent. Apart from anything else, this will reduce the proof-reading task later.

2. Identify the purpose of the document.

3. Identify the target readers and their likely expectations of the document on the formal/informal dimension.

4. Identify the image that you want the document to project.

5. Make decisions about the document's look horizontally. Remember that your choice of column combinations should relate to 2, 3 and 4 above. Having decided on the fundamental look, choose a typical page of your document and start to experiment with the column widths, fonts, leading, heading styles, etc. (Combining your knowledge from Parts 2, 3 and 4.)

6. When you are satisfied that the general horizontal layout meets your requirements, you can turn your attention to the vertical dimension. Begin with the first page of text: fit text, tables, headers, footers, and any ruled lines and illustrations onto the pages. The vertical look affects the *neatness* of each page and therefore the whole document.

7. If your document requires it, add a table of contents, an index, a cover page, etc.

8. Print the preliminary version.

9. Proof-read, marking all the improvements you want to make. Attend to the text itself, alignment of items and line ends. (Just mark on your copy where the line ends need managing, but decide *how*, at the next stage, on screen.) A tip for proof-reading is to read the text aloud, naming all the punctuation marks. This technique helps you slow down and see the text afresh.

10. Make the changes you have identified. (Even the smallest will be easy to spot if you have used a red pen.) Do a spell check and print the final draft. Re-check the layout, with particular attention to: the position of hyphens; the presence of danglers; the punctuation of bulleted lists.

11. Ideally, set the document aside for a few days and then look at it again — you will almost always see further improvements that can be made.

12. If possible, give the document to someone else to proof-read.

13. Make final changes and print the finished version.

14. After the document is produced, make a note of people who point out any errors to you. You can ask them to proof-read your next document!

Enjoy applying your new skills and remember that they will improve with each impressive document you produce.

House styles

Many organisations have a preferred style of layout (house style) to which people producing documents are expected to conform.

If you are the person determining the house style, changing it should be easy. As a help, you can provide people working in the organisation with copies of this book.

When the house style has been determined by a person unaware of the principles contained in the book, this may present a problem (depending on the character of that person) for someone who wishes to produce impressive documents.

The most direct approach is to share the book with them and to discuss ideas that you may have for improving the house style.

If you think you are likely to meet resistance, make a start by improving your documents using the principles in *Quick Bits*. Be patient. In time, people will notice that your documents look better and this may open up opportunities to suggest improvements.

If you meet lots of resistance at an early stage — if, for example, it is insisted that you underline headings — you have to approach making changes in a more structured and subtle way. Make a list of all the features of the current house style that you dislike and identify the one you think easiest to change. Start to mount a gentle campaign to bring about that improvement. Once you have succeeded, tackle the next on the list, and so on. With each success, subsequent change should be easier and more rapid.

Part 6. Worked Examples

On the following pages you will find examples of:

- Two leaflets.
- A return-slip on a letter.
- An overhead projector slide.
- A document cover.
- A document page.

Leaflets

Reproduced opposite is a leaflet based, as close as I dare, on an actual A5 leaflet from a restaurant. The outer line is just to indicate the overall size.

Three different fonts are used, Times Roman being the most common, used in *ten* combinations of size and style! Playbill and Impact are the other two fonts, both are in different sizes to any of the others. To add to the effect, the border, 'Special offer', 'Half price' and 'Starting from...' were printed in red.

This approach is said to be typical of people new to publishing using a computer and comes close to what is called a 'ransom note effect' (as when words of different fonts and sizes are cut from newspaper headlines).

Turn the page to see an alternative layout.

A WARM WELCOME
TO

Bumbleton
Chekkers Restaurant
Join in with our

SPECIAL OFFER

HALF PRICE

MAIN MEAL ONLY

(Eat in or Takeaway)

Advance Booking

STARTING FROM 25TH FEB

SUNDAY TO THURSDAY

UNTIL FURTHER NOTICE

HALF PRICE CASH OR CHEQUE ONLY

This offer applies to the Chekkers Restaurant ONLY

123 BUMBLE STREET

BUMBLETON

BUMBLESHIRE BQ44 3AA

TEL (0122X) 274X2X Or 27X7X7

OPEN 7 DAYS A WEEK

12.00 noon 2.30pm & 6.00pm to 11.30pm

The design decisions are based on the assumption that the restaurant owners would prefer to project a more ordered image as the food in the restaurant is not such a mish-mash! The items of information have been rearranged into a more logical sequence, which invited their re-writing.

First, the *Quick Bits* lessons have been applied. Particularly note the time formats and non-use of capitals for emphasis. The other design decisions were: to use one font; to drop the border in favour of the chequered flags found in the clipart that came with my word processor; and, to get away from centre-aligning everything, to put the information on the offer and the restaurant address into two table columns, separated by a rule.

The important message, the half-price offer, is put into the largest size (55 points) and the sequence is rearranged to put the essential 'half-price' first and ensure that the longer 'special offer!' line is at the bottom of the arrangement, giving it stability. The second most important message, the name of the restaurant, is second in size (20 points) and the rest of the text is in 13 points. The font chosen is Albertus. In the large point sizes its decorative character can be seen and, in the smaller ones, its roots as a modern style serif font come to the fore, making it reasonably easy to read. In each of the point sizes the leading is reduced because at normal single spacing the text did not hang together so well. This is a good example of improving legibility by reducing the space between lines when using large point sizes.

The visual impact of the offer and the chequered flags is increased (and attention therefore drawn to the leaflet) by the amount of white space around them.

The overall effect is modern and clean. If an old style serif font had been chosen it would have sent out the impression of an old-fashioned restaurant which might have been at odds with the giving of half-price offers. A script font, strongly associated with the style of expensive restaurants, would have been even more out of place.

Half-price special offer!

There is now even more reason for you to enjoy the warm welcome at

Bumbleton Chekkers Restaurant

You can enjoy a main meal to eat-in or take-away, at half price, from Sunday to Thursday if you order in advance and pay by cash or cheque.

This offer applies to Chekkers Restaurant only, from 25 February until further notice.

Chekkers Restaurant
123 Bumble Street
Bumbleton
Bumbleshire BQ44 3A
Tel: 0122X 274X2X
or 27X7X7

We are open seven days a week:
12.00 – 2.30 p.m. and
6.00 – 11.30 p.m.

Finally, with this version, I experimented with re-aligning the headline and graphic elements to get further away from the centred look. The heading had to be reduced to 50 points to make it fit that half of the table, but the flags could be correspondingly increased in size. It can be argued that the strong chequered flag pattern and the 'X' formed by the handles dominate the leaflet to the detriment of the text. However, if this leaflet is to be distributed, like the original, in a free paper, anything that grabs and holds the attention increases the likelihood that the leaflet will not be thrown away unread.

When looking at the previous page, did you notice that the lines above 'Bumbleton Chekkers Restaurant' are left-justified? The word 'the' was actually brought onto the following line with a non-breaking space because when it was on the end of the first line, it was less obviously left-justified. It has also had the effect of making 'enjoy' more prominent.

If the chequered flag motif did not fit with the restaurant name, a food-oriented graphic could have been used.

Turn back to the leaflet on which this was based and look at it afresh as your perspective will have now changed.

Half-price special offer!

There is now even more reason for you to enjoy the warm welcome at

Bumbleton Chekkers Restaurant

You can enjoy a main meal to eat-in or take-away, at half price, from Sunday to Thursday if you order in advance and pay by cash or cheque.

This offer applies to Chekkers Restaurant only, from 25 February until further notice.

Chekkers Restaurant
123 Bumble Street
Bumbleton
Bumbleshire BQ44 3AA
Tel: 0122X 274X2X
or 27X7X7

We are open seven days a week:
12.00 – 2.30 p.m. and
6.00 – 11.30 p.m.

The example opposite is adapted from the front of the type of leaflet where a landscape oriented A4 sheet is printed in three columns and folded between the columns to open as either a concertina or gate as illustrated below.

When you looked at the general layout, did it remind you of the comments about how people scan pages? (See pages 116 – 117.)

The leaflet uses varied letterspacing to fill out each line. The technique works best with short messages and if at least one word occupies a whole line. As with kerning letters, the delicate adjustment of leading is best done by eye.

A variant of this technique is to maintain normal letterspacing but to alter the font height until the word(s) fit the line. This can have a dramatic effect when the words per line vary considerably in length, and therefore in height. It is intensified when used with no additional leading, so that the words 'sit' on each other, as here.

message has been the same: you are finite

When doing fancy things to text it is more important than usual not to mix fonts, as the effect can easily slide into a mess. If you start collecting leaflets and look at magazine pages with new eyes, you will note that professional graphic designers sometimes break the 'rules' for effect. Remember that they know what they are doing, and why.

Folded A4 leaflets:

Concertina

Gate

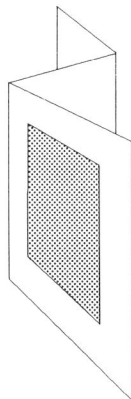

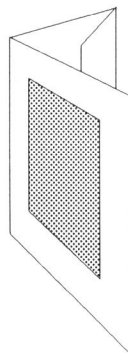

Throughout history the message has been the same:

You are finite but the infinite is within you...

Return-slip on a letter

The top example opposite is based on an actual return-slip from the bottom of a school letter.

The example below shows how it could be improved using *Impressive Documents* principles. As well as obvious things such as changing the capitalisation and underlining, note the vertical management of space and the re-aligned horizontal elements. The lines on which to write have been changed from broken underlining in the original, to a line produced by right-hand tabs with a dotted line leader. They now sit on the baseline of the text.

Most people realise when they see a choice of things and boxes by the side that they are expected to tick one, and dropping the 'tick box' request made it easier to line things up. It did seem a pity to remove the unintentional humour from the original instruction about writing the cheque, though!

- -

Design/Technology/Art Contributions

Name of Child _____ Class _____

I enclose a contribution of: ☐ £1.50 for 1 term
☐ £4.50 for the year (please tick box)

Please make cheques payable to BUMBLESHIRE COUNTY COUNCIL with your address on the back. Thank you.

Signed _____ Parent / Guardian

- -

Design/Technology/Art Contributions

Child's name .... Class ....

I enclose a contribution of: £1.50 for one term *or* ☐
£4.50 for whole year ☐

Make cheques payable to *Bumbleshire County Council*.
Please write your address on the back. Thank you.

Signed .... Parent/Guardian

Overhead projector slide

Overhead projector (OHP) slides can present problems for several reasons:

- The author may try to squeeze too much onto each slide.
- People who are asked to type the slides often do not see their results projected and are not therefore able to judge the effect.

The example opposite is based on a genuine slide, but half-size for clarity. In a naïve attempt to make the text clear, the author used capitals and allowed lots of space between the items. You will recall that text in capitals is less legible than ordinary mixed text. The use of large spaces made it hard to display the bottom items simultaneously with the heading.

VARICOSE VEIN TREATMENT

SEVERE CASES

SCLEROTHERAPY

* VEIN INJECTED
* COMPRESSION BANDAGE
* VEIN SCARRED AND BLOCKED

STRIPPING

* GENERAL ANAESTHETIC
* VEIN STRIPPED OUT OF LEG

INVERTED STRIPPING

* LOCAL ANAESTHETIC
* SMALL INCISIONS
* SECTIONS OF VEIN REMOVED WITH HOOK
* BANDAGES REMOVED IN DAYS, NO SCARRING

MINOR CASES

* ELASTIC SUPPORT STOCKINGS OR TIGHTS
* AVOID STANDING FOR LONG PERIODS
* TREAT CONSTIPATION
* REST WITH FEET UP

On revision, the slide has been divided in two and the orientation changed from portrait to landscape, which makes it easier for the presenter to manipulate. In order to fit both onto the opposite page they have been reduced to quarter-size.

The text has been put into a sans serif font and made as large as possible while leaving sufficient space for legibility and as margins.

The top slide uses word processing alone and the second incorporates a background such as can now often be found in Windows software or in a presentation manager program such as Microsoft PowerPoint, Lotus Freelance or Harvard Graphics. Using a background can give all the slides in the presentation a consistent look, but thought should be given to relate it to the audience and subject matter.

Varicose Vein Treatment
Severe cases

Sclerotherapy
- vein injected
- compression bandage
- vein scarred and blocked

Stripping
- general anaesthetic
- vein stripped out of leg

Inverted stripping
- local anaesthetic
- small incisions
- sections of vein removed with hook
- bandages removed in days, no scarring

Varicose Vein Treatment

Minor cases

- elastic support stockings or tights
- avoid standing for long periods
- treat constipation
- rest with feet up

Document cover

Document covers give great scope for the use of imagination and creativity. The example opposite is typical of one that, being justified to the centre and with its use of capitals, lacks these qualities.

ANALYSIS OF SALES POTENTIAL IN 'PACIFIC RIM' COUNTRIES

PETER JOHNSON
SALES MANAGER

The revised cover opposite is just one of many possible variations, but illustrates what can be done in only a few minutes, with a little thought.

The title is rearranged because in short messages it is a good idea to put the most important point first, as with 'half-price' on the restaurant leaflet example.

Flashy graphics are not necessary. The dart shape that both 'underlines' and draws attention to the title was simply drawn with the word processor's drawing facility.

Note that the text now fits into a rectangular frame. The title is justified to the left and the author's name and job title justified to the right. The two top points of the dart align with the edges of the rectangle and the lower point juts out slightly to the left. By doing so, it adds a dynamic note and leads the eye into the block. If the main block were not regular, this dynamic element would loose its impact.

I used a heavy font with thick downstrokes for the title and a contrasting sans serif font set in italics for the author's name and title.

Peter Johnson may be a dynamic manager, but you would not guess it from the first example.

Sales potential:
Analysis of
'Pacific Rim' countries

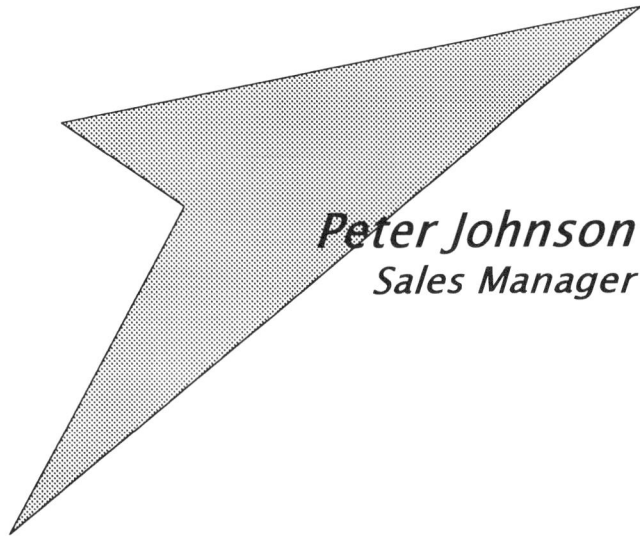

Peter Johnson
Sales Manager

Document page

Except for the page number, the page opposite reproduces *as I received it,* a page from a document that I then prepared for print for Bexley and Greenwich Health, with whose kind permission the following examples are produced. The document is a report on the experience and views of black and ethnic minority people with mental health problems. The audience for the document is the general public, mental health professionals, managers and executives of interested organisations. A fairly high degree of formality was therefore required, without sacrificing legibility or visual interest.

The example is used to illustrate, over a number of pages, the stages of development of the layout of a typical document.

Study it carefully and think about the changes you would make before you turn the page.

4.5   Counselling

Interviewees' knowledge of talking therapies raise a number of important issues. Many of those who were not involved in talking therapies were either ambiguous about what this involved or were unable to relate its value in terms of their own treatment and rehabilitation. Objections to therapeutic counselling can arise from service users' negative personal experience of statutory psychiatric services, such as compulsory admission or racial stereotyping.   The small number of interviewees who had received counselling described the experience as negative and pointed to the tendency of psychologists to stereotype Africans and African-Caribbeans at the expense of making individual assessments.   One interviewee perceived racial stereotyping as meaning his psychologist often *invented problems I did not have*.   Another suggested that his psychiatrist found it hard to communicate with him because *I am an articulate black man.*

Everyone who currently receives therapeutic counselling (3) described their experiences as positive. However, the survey sample is too small to significantly assess the overall impact and outcomes of therapeutic counselling on the rehabilitation of African and African-Caribbean service users in Greenwich.   A further enquiry of a larger number of users would have to be undertaken to provide a more thorough appraisal.

There is very little research on health promotion and its impact on the uptake of services by black and minority ethnic communities. However research on access to services by black and minority ethnic communities suggests that basic lack of awareness and information about services, racism (overt or indirect) and communication difficulties
can have a detrimental affect on service uptake. A recent Department of Health publication on ethnicity and health, states that the uptake of services by people from black and minority ethnic communities is affected by access to services, encounters with services, lifestyle and cultural practices and socio-economic status[1] . The impact of these factors on the under representation of interviewees on therapeutic counselling programmes should be considered by purchasers and service providers.

> Lack of information about counselling services has prevented a number of service users from accessing these services. Service providers must do more to ensure that information about these services is available and accessible to black service users. This could take the form of more proactive outreach work and/or specific targeting of African and African-Caribbean service users. The findings suggest that dislike of a particular service, based on negative personal experience, can engender negative attitudes towards similar services and the staff who provide them. A report into black and minority ethnic communities' access to mental health care supports these findings, that if services are perceived to be coercive (i.e. compulsory detention), then service users are less likely to seek further treatment[2] .

---

[1]   Department of Health, *Ethnicity and Health - a Guide for the NHS*; London 1993.
[2]   Lipsedge Maurice, *Mental Health: access to care for black and ethnic minority people*. In: Hopkins A., Bahl V., eds. Access to health care for people from Black and ethnic minorities. London: Royal College of Physicians, 1993.

There are some elements in the original that I dealt with first, in *Quick Bits* fashion:

- In the header, four full stops instead of an ellipsis symbol.
- Double spaces after full stops.
- The lack of punctuation around the quotations at the end of the first paragraph made them look at first as if the italics were being used for emphasis. I therefore decided to enclose them in single quotation marks instead.
- The numeral three by itself in the middle of the page. In removing this, I re-wrote the text slightly.
- In the third paragraph:
  — Unnaturally short line in the third paragraph owing to a stray 'enter'.
  — After 'detrimental', 'affect' should be 'effect' — this is one of those mistakes like 'principal' and 'principle'.
  — Unnecessary comma after 'ethnicity and health'.
  — Footnote number inside the full stop. (Also in box.)

I then removed the shading in the header and the box. I did this because shading produced by a laser printer at 600 dots per inch looks unpleasant when compared with grey shading used by printers, who can produce a very fine effect at thousands of dots per inch. The line around the box was supposed to be a 'shadow box' but the variation was not very distinct, so I increased it. The lines of the box were also 'tight' to the text, giving it a mean appearance.

The first stage of experimentation with changes, illustrated opposite, shows that I quickly settled on a format of two columns of un-even width. In part, this was to produce a shorter (and therefore easier to read) line for the 12 point text and in part it was because other sections of the document did not have boxes and I could leave the narrow column blank where necessary. I changed the justification and improved the inter-paragraph and below-heading space.

I also reduced the size of the header and located it over the narrow column. I did not, however, change it from italics and capitals, thus breaking two 'rules'. Now that the header was rather small, I wanted to increase its strength as a visual element. I felt that the alternative, using bold, would clash with the heading and text in the box. Perhaps there are better solutions?

The original general font was GC Times which, whilst having a less severe appearance than Times New Roman, is still not as round, and therefore pleasant to the eye as Charter, which I ended up using. I stayed with Arial in bold for the heading font (increased from 12 to 13 points) and also used 10 point Arial in the box. This restored some of the contrast lost with the shading.

At 12 points with automatic line spacing, the main text flowed over to the top of the right-hand column. My first thought was to separate the two with a ruled line. Note too that at this stage I had the automatic hyphenation turned on, which produced some untoward effects including the part-word 'dangler' above the box. The hyphenation within the box is itself appalling.

4.5 Counselling

Interviewees' knowledge of talking therapies raise a number of issues. Many of those who were not involved in such therapies were either uncertain about what they involve or were unable to relate their value in terms of their own treatment and rehabilitation. Objections to therapeutic counselling can arise from service users' negative personal experience of statutory psychiatric services, such as compulsory admission or racial stereotyping. The small number of interviewees who had received counselling described the experience as negative and pointed to the tendency of psychologists to stereotype Africans and African-Caribbeans at the expense of making individual assessments. One interviewee perceived racial stereotyping as meaning his psychologist 'often invented problems I did not have.' Another suggested that his psychiatrist found it hard to communicate with him 'because I am an articulate black man'.

The three interviewees who currently receive therapeutic counselling described their experiences as positive. However, the survey sample is too small to significantly assess the overall impact and outcomes of therapeutic counselling on the rehabilitation of African and African-Caribbean service users in Greenwich. A further enquiry of a larger number of users would have to be undertaken to provide a more thorough appraisal.

There is very little research on health promotion and its impact on the uptake of services by black and minority ethnic communities. However research on access to services by black and minority ethnic communities suggests that basic lack of awareness and information about services, racism (overt or indirect) and communication difficulties can have a detrimental effect on service uptake. A recent Department of Health publication on ethnicity and health states that the uptake of services by people from black and minority ethnic communities is affected by access to services, encounters with services, lifestyle, cultural practices and socio-economic status.[1] The impact of these factors on the under representation of interviewees on therapeutic counselling programmes should be considered by purchasers and service providers.

Lack of information about counselling services has prevented a number of service users from accessing these services. Service providers must do more to ensure that information about these services is available and accessible to black service users. This could take the form of more proactive outreach work and/or specific targeting of African and African-Caribbean service users. The findings suggest that dislike of a particular service, based on negative personal experience, can engender negative attitudes towards similar services and the staff who provide them. A report into black and minority ethnic communities' access to mental health care supports these findings. If services are perceived to be coercive (e.g. compulsory detention) then service users are less likely to seek further treatment.[2]

---

[1] Department of Health, *Ethnicity and Health — a Guide for the NHS*; London 1993.

[2] Lipsedge Maurice, Mental Health: Access to care for black and ethnic minority people. In: Hopkins A., Bahl V., eds. Access to health care for people from black and ethnic minorities. London: Royal College of Physicians, 1993.

The next step was to turn my attention to the characteristics of the text rather than the general layout.

The automatic hyphenation went first. Then the main text was put into 10.5 points and the line spacing was fixed at 14 points for both the general and box text which, you will recall, was 10 points tall. The slightly-more-than-normal leading in the sans serif Arial text, enhances its legibility and, by using the same line spacing for both sets of text, they are better aligned (until, at least, the left-hand text has a paragraph break).

Thinking again about the layout, I centred the box vertically above the footnote in the now vacant column and changed the shadow box outline to a simple one.

4.5 Counselling

Interviewees' knowledge of talking therapies raise a number of issues. Many of those who were not involved in such therapies were either uncertain about what they involve or were unable to relate their value in terms of their own treatment and rehabilitation. Objections to therapeutic counselling can arise from service users' negative personal experience of statutory psychiatric services, such as compulsory admission or racial stereotyping. The small number of interviewees who had received counselling described the experience as negative and pointed to the tendency of psychologists to stereotype Africans and African-Caribbeans at the expense of making individual assessments. One interviewee perceived racial stereotyping as meaning his psychologist 'often invented problems I did not have.' Another suggested that his psychiatrist found it hard to com-municate with him 'because I am an articulate black man'.

The three interviewees who currently receive therapeutic counselling described their experiences as positive. However, the survey sample is too small to significantly assess the overall impact and outcomes of therapeutic counselling on the rehabilitation of African and African-Caribbean service users in Greenwich. A further enquiry of a larger number of users would have to be undertaken to provide a more thorough appraisal.

There is very little research on health promotion and its impact on the uptake of services by black and minority ethnic communities. However research on access to services by black and minority ethnic communities suggests that basic lack of awareness and information about services, racism (overt or indirect) and communication difficulties can have a detrimental effect on service uptake. A recent Department of Health publication on ethnicity and health states that the uptake of services by people from black and minority ethnic communities is affected by access to services, encounters with services, lifestyle, cultural practices and socio-economic status.[1] The impact of these factors on the under represent-ation of interviewees on therapeutic counselling programmes should be considered by purchasers and service providers.

> **Lack of information about counselling services has prevented a number of service users from accessing these services. Service providers must do more to ensure that information about these services is available and accessible to black service users. This could take the form of more proactive outreach work and/or specific targeting of African and African-Caribbean service users. The findings suggest that dislike of a particular service, based on negative personal experience, can engender negative attitudes towards similar services and the staff who provide them. A report into black and minority ethnic communities' access to mental health care supports these findings. If services are perceived to be coercive (e.g. compulsory detention) then service users are less likely to seek further treatment.[2]**

---

[1] Department of Health, *Ethnicity and Health — a Guide for the NHS*; London 1993.

[2] Lipsedge Maurice, Mental Health: Access to care for black and ethnic minority people. In: Hopkins A., Bahl V., eds. Access to health care for people from black and ethnic minorities. London: Royal College of Physicians, 1993.

Finally, for the finished version, the point size of the main text is increased to 11 points to make better use of the space and the first paragraph right-hand indentation was eased out 0.2mm to reduce the raggedness of the line ends and to move back onto the previous line the word 'man', which had become a 'dangler' with the change of font size. It only needed one hyphen in the final paragraph to prevent 'providers' from being a dangler too.

The rule between the columns was removed because the border around the box is now sufficient to separate it from the rest. The thickness of that line was reduced from 0.75 to 0.5 points to make it less intrusive. The top of the box was aligned with the top of the x-height line of the first paragraph.

The final touch was to reduce the point size of the footnotes and give them a 'hanging indent' so that the number is clear of the text.

Having established a satisfactory format for this page, I then applied it to the rest of the document.

4.5 Counselling

Interviewees' knowledge of talking therapies raise a number of issues. Many of those who were not involved in such therapies were either uncertain about what they involve or were unable to relate their value in terms of their own treatment and rehabilitation. Objections to therapeutic counselling can arise from service users' negative personal experience of statutory psychiatric services, such as compulsory admission or racial stereotyping. The small number of interviewees who had received counselling described the experience as negative and pointed to the tendency of psychologists to stereotype Africans and African-Caribbeans at the expense of making individual assessments. One interviewee perceived racial stereotyping as meaning his psychologist 'often invented problems I did not have.' Another suggested that his psychiatrist found it hard to communicate with him 'because I am an articulate black man'.

The three interviewees who currently receive therapeutic counselling described their experiences as positive. However, the survey sample is too small to significantly assess the overall impact and outcomes of therapeutic counselling on the rehabilitation of African and African-Caribbean service users in Greenwich. A further enquiry of a larger number of users would have to be undertaken to provide a more thorough appraisal.

There is very little research on health promotion and its impact on the uptake of services by black and minority ethnic communities. However research on access to services by black and minority ethnic communities suggests that basic lack of awareness and information about services, racism (overt or indirect) and communication difficulties can have a detrimental effect on service uptake. A recent Department of Health publication on ethnicity and health states that the uptake of services by people from black and minority ethnic communities is affected by access to services, encounters with services, lifestyle, cultural practices and socio-economic status.[1] The impact of these factors on the under representation of interviewees on therapeutic counselling programmes should be considered by purchasers and service providers.

> **Lack of information about counselling services has prevented a number of service users from accessing these services. Service providers must do more to ensure that information about these services is available and accessible to black service users. This could take the form of more proactive outreach work and/or specific targeting of African and African-Caribbean service users. The findings suggest that dislike of a particular service, based on negative personal experience, can engender negative attitudes towards similar services and the staff who provide them. A report into black and minority ethnic communities' access to mental health care supports these findings. If services are perceived to be coercive (e.g. compulsory detention) then service users are less likely to seek further treatment.[2]**

---

[1] Department of Health, *Ethnicity and Health — a Guide for the NHS*; London 1993.

[2] Lipsedge Maurice, *Mental Health: Access to care for black and ethnic minority people*. In: Hopkins A., Bahl V., eds. Access to health care for people from black and ethnic minorities. London: Royal College of Physicians, 1993.

Part 7. Test Yourself

The page opposite mimics in the layout and 'faults', a document produced by a large national organisation. It was, I thought, a valiant attempt to use the facilities of the word processor to get away from their previous dire document layout but it is let down by a lack of knowledge of the principles described in this book.

Without commenting on the wording, there are at least nineteen *Quick Bits* or layout changes that I would recommend. There may be other changes that *you* would make. How many can you identify before you turn the page?

4. Payments by Banker's Automated Credit

4.1   It is recommended that our regular suppliers are offered the possibility of receiving payments by Direct Credit. The use of BACS to make payments direct to Company bank aacounts will reduce our transaction and/or cheque handing costs. The benefits for our creditors will be:

- cleared funds in their account the same day that ours is debited;

- payments made accurately and quickly into any U.K. bank or building society;

- the cost of handling cheques eliminated;

- possibility of postal delays eliminated.

5. Security

5.1   Various safeguards are built into the system for us and for our creditors. We have identified four key components:

(i)   *Under our control*

The software to make these payments is linked to our general ledger system and is subject to the same strict security procedures and audit scrutiny[4].

(ii)   *Specialised reporting*

Special reports are produced weekly or monthly to enable the functioning of the system to be closely monitored.

(ii)   *Bank guarantees*

We determine the payments to be made and if errors occur in the <u>banking</u> system, the error is corrected and our transaction costs refunded.

(iii)   *Fall-back*

If the system fails, or if suppliers prefer it, cheques can still be issued as previously.

---

[4]   copies of the procedures are available from the Finance department.

4

From top to bottom, the points for improvement are:

1. Inter-paragraph spacing would benefit from being reduced.
2. This indentation is unnecessary.
3. Two spaces are used after full stops.
4. Incorrect capitalisation.
5. Spelling not checked.
6. Over-sized bullets disturb the look of the page.
7. The fully justified lines in bulleted lists look weak.
8. Dangler not dealt with.
9. Bulleted list adapted from a continuous list and therefore not correctly punctuated or appropriately capitalised.
10. Full stops used in abbreviation — not usual these days.
11. Mixed styles of lists.
12. Italics used in headings.
13. Indentation is appropriate, but the amount is excessive.
14. Automatic numbering not used.
15. Underlining used for emphasis instead of italics.
16. Poorly aligned footnote.
17. Footnote text is usually two points or so smaller than the main text but, at four points smaller, this is too small. Legibility is reduced and the footnote has also become too strong a visual element.
18. Capitals needed.
19. Page number font does not match the rest of the text. As the number is in *Courier* it appears to be 'left over' from the original font setting.

There is also, of course, the question of whether, overall, a single-column layout is most appropriate.

4. Payments by Banker's Automated Credit

4.1 It is recommended that our regular suppliers are offered the possibility of receiving payments by Direct Credit. ~~The use of BACS to make payments direct to~~ Company bank accounts will reduce our transaction and/or cheque handing costs. The benefits for our creditors will be:

- cleared funds in their account the same day that ours is debited;

- payments made accurately and quickly into any U.K. bank or building society;

- the cost of handling cheques eliminated;

- possibility of postal delays eliminated.

5. Security

5.1 Various safeguards are built into the system for us and for our creditors. We have identified four key components:

(i) *Under our control*

The software to make these payments is linked to our general ledger system and is subject to the same strict security procedures and audit scrutiny[4].

(ii) *Specialised reporting*

Special reports are produced weekly or monthly to enable the functioning of the system to be closely monitored.

(ii) *Bank guarantees*

We determine the payments to be made and if errors occur in the banking system, the error is corrected and our transaction costs refunded.

(iii) *Fall-back*

If the system fails, or if suppliers prefer it, cheques can still be issued as previously.

---

[4] copies of the procedures are available from the Finance department.

4

155

Part 8. Going Further

You may find it useful to keep a note of the main features of the documents you produce and, importantly, if you are to learn from your efforts, the positive and negative comments that people make about them.

I have therefore produced the page opposite, which you are welcome to photocopy and keep with your own copies of finished documents. While it will be tempting for you to photocopy other parts of this book, please respect the fact that you do *not* have permission to do so. Also, you will not be helping people to whom you pass the copies, as they will need to work through the whole book in order to benefit in the same way you have.

As you put what you have learned into practice you will find pleasure comparing your work with that of other people. Both good and bad examples of typography and graphic design will inspire you. You can often find excellent, up-to-date examples in magazines that come with Sunday papers and in promotional magazines published by large booksellers. Advertisements are a source of adventurous design. You will not need to look for examples of poor documents: unfortunately, they will confront you everywhere. If you pick up a document and your instant reaction is negative, pause a moment to analyse why. More often than not you will find that it is because the person who produced it has broken some of the basic principles about the choice of fonts and use of space.

I hope you have enjoyed your journey so far. Turning ordinary documents into *impressive* ones takes a little time but is very satisfying and, once you start, the journey never finishes...

Reading

If you want more detailed information on the topics covered in this book you will need to search it out from several sources. Fortunately, guides to vocabulary, correct grammar and punctuation are easy to find in bookshops and libraries. For books on typography and graphic design look under those topics or desktop publishing, where you will find plenty of variety. I have found the following books particularly useful:

- **Good Word Guide** edited by Martin Manser, published by Bloomsbury Publishing, 1991. ISBN 0 7475 0875 5. Currently out-of-print, but worth seeking out for its clear explanations of commonly misused words and phrases.
- **Guide to Written English** by James Aitchison, published by Cassell, 1994. ISBN 0 304 34314 5. Thorough on grammar, punctuation, styles of writing and planning written work.
- **Typography for Desktop Publishers** by Grant Shipcott. Published in the *Graphic Design for the Computer Age* series by Batsford, 1994. ISBN 0 7134 7212 X. Comprehensive, with has many inspiring examples. It also deals with using colour in documents.

Document record sheet

Name of document:

Author:

Date final version produced:

Purpose of document: Target readership:

Size and general layout (number of columns, etc.)

Table of styles used:

Style	Font	Point size	Leading (inter-line, before and after)	Justific-ation	Other
Normal (body text)			i b a		
Heading level 1			i b a		
Heading level 2			i b a		
Heading level 3			i b a		
Heading level 4			i b a		
Numbered or bulleted lists			i b a		
			i b a		
			i b a		
			i b a		

Unsolicited *positive* comments about the document.

Unsolicited *negative* comments about the document.

Glossary

Page numbers follow entries where appropriate. Words in italics refer to other entries.

Ampersand The '&' symbol. 41

Em dash A long dash (—). 18

En dash A short dash (–). 18

Font categories Groups of *Fonts* with similar characteristics, such as: Old Style Serif; *Sans Serif*; Modern Serif; Script; Decorative. 68

Font A set of characters of a particular design. 'Font' used to be restricted to mean a typeface in a particular size but the words are now used synonymously. 66

Font styles The variants of a *font* used for particular purposes. Font styles include: *roman*, italic, light and bold. 70

Footer Text, *rules*, etc., below the bottom margin. 114

Gutter The gap between columns. 80

Header Text, *rules*, etc., above the top margin. 114

Junk mail Rich source of examples of good and bad typography.

Justification Alignment of text to the left or right margin, both margins or the centre-line. (Also called flush left, flush right, fully justified and centred, respectively.) An unaligned text edge is *ragged*. 54

Kerning Adjustment to the space between pairs of letters — only needed with type in large *point* sizes. 86

Leading Space between lines of text. Pronounced 'ledding', as the name came from the metal lead used in setting metal type. Leading is measured in *points*. 88

Legibility The ease, or otherwise, with which a *font* can be read, unlike readability, which is whether or not the content of the text is interesting. 66

Loose Expanded *letterspacing*. 84

Letterspacing The horizontal space between characters. 84

Non-keyboard characters Characters that are not represented on the keyboard but are accessible by entering keystrokes or codes. 15

Non-printing characters Codes embedded in text as instructions to the word processor. In certain work modes, may be seen on the screen.

Paragraph style The defining *font*, indentation, *leading* and other characteristics of a paragraph. Paragraph styles can be named and saved in a document and used to quickly define or re-define the characteristics of new text, headings, etc. Extremely useful facility with a variety of names, depending on the producer of the software. 44

Point The usual measure of the height of printed characters and *leading*. One point is $1/72$ of an inch. 66

Proportional spacing Characters vary in width, e.g. 'm' is wider than 'j'. Contrasts with fixed-width characters (monospaced) typical of manual typewriters. 36

Ragged When the edge of a paragraph is not aligned. See *justification*. 54

Roman The 'normal' *font style*, that is, not bold or italic, etc. 70

Rule A straight line used as a graphic device and in place of underlining. 32, 108, 114

Sans Serif *Font category* where characters do not have *serifs*. 68

Serifs Small strokes at the extremities of characters. 68

Small caps Capital letters reduced to the *x-height* of the *font*. 28

Soft break A *non-printing character* that signals the end of the line without ending the paragraph. 62

Strong visual element A design feature on a page that attracts the reader's attention. 116, 118

Style Has several meanings: the overall look of a document; *paragraph styles*; *font styles*.

Tight Condensed *letterspacing*. 84

Tracking Same as *letterspacing*. 84

Typeface See *font*. 66

Typography The art of creating and working with type.

x-height Height of a lower case 'x'. A key determinant of the look of a font. 67

'The growth in availability of colour printers and photocopiers in offices will present new design problems.'

'You mean...the potential to produce unprofessional-looking documents will increase?'

Create Impressive Documents. Published by Briarwood 1000, Bury St Edmunds, England.